Michelle
Obama
In Her Own Words

Michelle Obama

In Her Own Words

EDITED BY

Marta Evans
and
Hannah Masters

A B2 BOOK

AGATE

CHICAGO

Printed in the United States of America

Library of Congress Cataloging-in-Publication Data

Names: Evans, Marta, editor. | Masters, Hannah, editor.
Title: Michelle Obama in her own words / edited by Marta Evans and Hannah
    Masters.
Description: Chicago : B2 Books, An Agate Imprint, [2021] | Summary: "A
    collection of more than 300 quotes from Michelle Obama, author, lawyer,
    humanitarian, and trailblazing first African American First Lady of the
    United States of America"-- Provided by publisher.
Identifiers: LCCN 2020051911 (print) | LCCN 2020051912 (ebook) | ISBN
    9781572842953 (paperback) | ISBN 9781572848511 (ebook)
Subjects: LCSH: Obama, Michelle, 1964- | Obama, Michelle,
    1964---Quotations. | African American women
    lawyers--Illinois--Chicago--Quotations. | Presidents' spouses--United
    States--Quotations. | Legislators' spouses--United States--Quotations.
Classification: LCC E909 .M53 2021 (print) | LCC E909 (ebook) | DDC
    973.932092--dc23
LC record available at https://lccn.loc.gov/2020051911
LC ebook record available at https://lccn.loc.gov/2020051912

10 9 8 7 6 5 4 3 2 1   21 22 23 24 25

B2 Books is an imprint of Agate Publishing. Agate books are available in bulk at discount prices. For more information, go to agatepublishing.com.

At fifty-four, I am still in progress, and I hope that I always will be. For me, becoming isn't about arriving somewhere or achieving a certain aim. I see it instead as forward motion, a means of evolving, a way to reach continuously toward a better self. The journey doesn't end.

— MICHELLE OBAMA

Contents

Introduction

Michelle Obama is optimistic about America—though she would be the first to admit it's not always an easy attitude to maintain. As the first Black First Lady of the United States, she had a unique vantage point from which to witness what America is capable of, both good and bad. With a family history that traces a line from slavery through emancipation and the Great Migration to the pinnacle of power in the United States, her story reflects tragic American injustices alongside the American hope of overcoming them.

In 1964 on Chicago's South Side, Michelle LaVaughn Robinson was born to Marian Robinson, a secretary, and Fraser Robinson III, a city water plant worker who put in long hours despite struggling with multiple sclerosis. The family was working-class and lived in a small apartment where Michelle and her older brother Craig shared a room split by a wooden divider. It was a childhood full of warmth and freedom, with long days spent playing outside and a tradition of family meals. Marian and Fraser encouraged the children to explore and ask questions. Michelle recalls demanding why she had to eat eggs for breakfast, which she didn't like. When her parents said it was because she needed protein, she lobbied, strategically, for peanut butter and jelly sandwiches as a replacement—and won.

Her parents were frank about what it would take for a Black girl like Michelle to succeed—that along with her talent and intelligence, she would need exceptional perseverance to reach her goals. The Robinsons set their expectations high, both for her schoolwork and her responsibilities to her family and community. Michelle, who took her parents' work ethic as a model, read by age four and was enrolled in a gifted program by sixth grade. She went on to attend Chicago's first public magnet high school, where she was a member of the National Honor Society and served as student council treasurer.

Her diligence paid off. Despite the doubts of at least one college counselor, who told Michelle "I'm not sure you're Princeton material," she graduated as the salutatorian and was admitted to Princeton with a work-study scholarship. There, though she excelled in class, she often felt alienated at the majority-white school and sought refuge in her connections to the small group of other Black students. She carried these experiences with her to Harvard Law School, where she worked to increase diversity on campus.

After Harvard, Michelle returned to Chicago and took a position at the prestigious law firm Sidley Austin. Soon she was assigned to mentor a summer associate named Barack Obama. Barack showed immediate interest in her, but she always declined, wary of dating a coworker. When she finally agreed to a date, the relationship quickly grew serious. Three years later, they were married.

Michelle, who had begun to question her satisfaction with corporate law, left the firm for public service roles in city government and nonprofits. These changes were due partly to Barack's encouragement to take risks and pursue her interests. But it was also the loss of her father, who died in 1991 at age 55, that caused her to reconsider her priorities. Her father had taught her the value of keeping your word and showing up for other people. She wanted to honor his memory by keeping these values at the center of her life and work.

Barack, in his own search for meaningful work, had set his sights on politics. Michelle was less than thrilled. She had a long-held skepticism about politicians, whom she felt acted mainly out of self-interest. But she trusted Barack and didn't want to stand in his way. Cautiously, she supported him through his successful campaign for Illinois State Senate in 1996.

The demands of Barack's political schedule became more difficult after the birth of their first daughter, Malia, in 1998. Three years after their second daughter, Sasha, was born in 2001, as Barack eyed a United States Senate seat, Michelle made him promise that if he lost the race, he would get out of politics altogether. But he didn't lose. Michelle juggled her own career with caring for the children in Chicago while Barack commuted to Washington. As his popularity increased following a speech at the 2004 Democratic National Convention, Michelle was swayed by the idea that the truths he stood for could be put into action on the national political stage. Even so, she agreed to his presidential campaign without really believing he would win.

As she scaled back her career to accompany Barack on the campaign trail, Michelle's own fame grew. Though many voters responded to her humor and honesty, she was intensely scrutinized by the press and political opponents. Animosity has always been present in politics, but race played a large role in the attacks levied against the Obamas, which often implicitly—and sometimes explicitly—painted Michelle as the stereotype of the "angry Black woman." Nevertheless, with the support of a broad and energetic coalition of voters, the Obamas were carried to the White House.

Michelle Obama carefully considered what kind of First Lady she would be. Despite the pressures of the public eye, she made it her mission to continue to present her authentic self. Aspects that made her unusual among first ladies—her race, her working-class upbringing, her prominent career path, her education (she was the third First Lady in history with a graduate degree)— allowed her to speak in a personal way to women of color, working mothers, girls who dreamed big, families who struggled to make ends meet, and so many others. Her two young daughters were always her priority in the White House, and being "mom-in-chief" also informed her public projects. The Let's Move! initiative, which aimed to provide children with access to and education about nutritious food, arose from the memory of her own difficulties ensuring Malia and Sasha had healthy meals while she worked full-time. Similarly, through Let Girls Learn, she connected her hopes for her daughters' education to educational justice work for girls all over the world.

During her time in the White House, Michelle Obama's approval ratings often outstripped her husband's. As a private citizen, her popularity has remained high. In her memoir, *Becoming*, she shared her successes and struggles in more detail, hoping her story would be an inspiration. Despite being repeatedly nudged toward a political career, her focus remains on serving the public outside of elected office, by lending her name to get out the vote campaigns and starting new initiatives to fight for the causes close to her heart. Michelle carries no illusions about the difficulty of making change, especially for those whom society leaves most vulnerable. But she argues that it is precisely for this reason that optimism is a commitment worth making—that our faith in a better future is what helps us achieve it.

Part I

PERSONAL LIFE

I Had Nothing or I Had Everything

Growing Up in Chicago

CHICAGO IS THE city that taught me what it means to give back.

—Instagram, May 31, 2019

EVEN THOUGH OUR family was crammed into a tiny apartment, one of the greatest gifts [my mom] gave me was the freedom to explore and develop into my own person.

—Instagram, May 10, 2019

DANDY AND GRANDMA raised a beautiful family of five children, and to this day, their stories are woven together with my own; their sacrifices and successes are braided into everything I've become.

—Instagram, September 8, 2019

MY FATHER GAVE us absolutely everything. The laughs and lessons, the hugs, the heartache from losing him—they're all still there with me, every minute.

—Instagram, April 14, 2019

YEAH, I WENT to Princeton and Harvard, but the lens through which I see the world is the lens that I grew up with. I am the product of a working-class upbringing. I grew up on the South Side of Chicago in a working-class community.

—"Michelle Obama on Elitism," *The New York Times*, April 15, 2008

[GRANDMA] WAS PERHAPS my first example of a professional woman, showing me that being graceful and being in command weren't mutually exclusive.

—Instagram, September 8, 2019

TOGETHER, IN OUR cramped apartment on the South Side of Chicago, my family helped me see the value in our story, in my story, and in the larger story of our country.

—**Instagram, May 22, 2018**

EVERY PARENT'S FIRST job is to keep their kids safe. But sometimes that instinct can get out of hand. . . . No one understood that better than my mother, Marian Robinson. She gave my brother, Craig, and me the freedom to roam—not just in our neighborhood, but within our own minds and burgeoning moral codes.

—***The National*, Amtrak, August/September 2019**

FOR AS LONG as I can remember, my big brother Craig has always had my back. He's still one of my best friends today.

—**Instagram, April 10, 2019**

MY BROTHER AND I shared a bedroom that was divided in half by a wooden partition, giving us each our own little tiny rooms that fit just a twin bed and a small desk. So we didn't have much space, but we had a whole lot of love.

—Let Girls Learn in London, June 16, 2015

WE WOULD PLAY outside all day long, from morning until the street lights came on.

—"First Lady: Nation's Health 'Starts With Our Kids',"
Talk of the Nation, June 12, 2012

WHEN I WAS still in elementary school, my dad bought my brother a pair of boxing gloves. But when he came home from the store, he was carrying not one, but two pairs of gloves. He wasn't going to teach his son to punch without making sure his daughter could throw a left hook, too.

—*Vogue*, July 29, 2019

FROM AN EARLY age, [my mom] saw that I had a flame inside me, and she never tempered it. She made sure that I could keep it lit.

—Instagram, May 12, 2019

WHEN I SAW my grandparents and heard about their sacrifice, my notion was, 'Oh, little girl, you better get that gold star. They're counting on you.'

—*O, The Oprah Magazine*, December 2018

WE CONSTANTLY FELT the struggle to balance our family responsibilities and the schoolwork, the activities, and the goals that we had for ourselves. And through it all, my parents fully expected us to do both—to achieve our dreams, and be there for our family.

—Let Girls Learn in London, June 16, 2015

MY PARENTS TOLD me every day I could do anything—I could grow up to be a doctor, a lawyer, a scientist, whatever—but only if I worked as hard as I could to succeed in school.

—**Let Girls Learn in London, June 16, 2015**

OUR VOICES HAD real value in our house. There's some people who raise kids and they use the philosophy 'kids are to be seen and not heard,' and it was just the opposite for us.

—**"Meet the Author: Michelle Obama," Virgin, December 11, 2018**

AS MY MOTHER used to say, 'Sometimes you just need to get out there and live your life, and have your mistakes where I can't see them, because I'm tired of watching you walk into the wall.'

—**"Oprah's 2020 Vision Tour Visionaries: Michelle Obama Interview," February 12, 2020**

WHEN I THINK of [Euclid Avenue, Chicago], when I think of our childhood, I think of music. Music was the backdrop of everything. We didn't do anything without music, and that's because our father was a big jazz lover and had a huge jazz album collection that he cherished.

—"Growing Up Robinson with Craig and Michelle," *The Michelle Obama Podcast*, August 19, 2020

THE MUSIC OF Motown is one of the great joys of my life—I love the soul, the beat, the energy.

—Twitter, December 12, 2019

DID YOU KNOW that Stevie Wonder is my favorite?

—Carpool Karaoke, *The Late Late Show with James Corden*, July 20, 2016

WHAT I SAW in our father was that nothing replaces getting on the phone and calling somebody, showing up for somebody.

—"Growing Up Robinson with Craig and Michelle," *The Michelle Obama Podcast*, August 19, 2020

THERE WERE VICTORY gardens everywhere. Families that were poor—folks that came from large families, like my parents, where there were six, seven kids each—you relied heavily on those gardens to incorporate vegetables. And that was a tradition.

—*Cooking Light*, February 6, 2015

MY DAD WAS a shift worker, so there were some dinner times when he was at work, but whenever he was there we would sit around the table with the plastic tablecloth, and that's when we would catch up and we'd talk about what we were eating, talk about what was going on in the day.

—*Cooking Light*, February 6, 2015

MY BROTHER HAS been my hero from day one.

—**"Michelle Obama says her brother is still their mother's favorite,"** *Good Morning America*, **November 13, 2018**

[CRAIG'S] LIKE 6'6". He's my big brother, and it's hard to be much taller than me, but I look up to my brother.

—**"Michelle Obama on Childhood Fire Drills and Taming Barack Obama's Tardiness,"** *The Tonight Show*, **December 19, 2018**

I ADORED MY brother. I have been 'Craig Robinson's little sister' for most of my life. And I could have an attitude about it, but I am a fan too.

—**"Michelle Obama says her brother is still their mother's favorite,"** *Good Morning America*, **November 13, 2018**

UNLIKE MY MOM, we didn't learn how to cook. That wasn't something my mother stressed for me. We came from the generation where my mom wanted me to go to college and law school, and she always said, 'You'll learn how to cook,' but that's not something she pressed.

—*Cooking Light*, **February 6, 2015**

MY DAD, HE'S our rock. To grow up with a dad with a disability, who never complained, went to work every day, didn't miss a day of work. Never remember Dad being sick or talking about being sick. When you grow up with that kind of drive and those values, we just never wanted to disappoint him.

—"**Michelle Obama says her brother is still their mother's favorite,**" *Good Morning America*, **November 13, 2018**

I AM AND always will be a Robinson. That means a lot of things, but maybe most of all, it means I show my love by sharing stories. We are a soulful, boisterous bunch of South Siders, always at our best when crowded around a kitchen table, cracking jokes and catching each other up on the ups and downs of our lives.

—*The National*, **Amtrak, August/September 2019**

I GREW UP with a disabled dad in a too-small house with not much money in a starting-to-fail neighborhood, and I also grew up surrounded by love and music in a diverse city in a country where an education can take you far. I had nothing or I had everything. It depends on which way you want to tell it.

—*Becoming*, **p. 416, November 2018**

CHICAGO MADE ME who I am.

—**Instagram, November 13, 2018**

Education & Career

I CAN TELL you that from the South Side of
Chicago to Princeton and Harvard and beyond,
my education unlocked so many doors for me.

—**Instagram, May 2, 2018**

IT WAS CLEAR to me that nobody was going to
take my hand and lead me to where I needed to
go. Instead, it was going to be up to me to reach
my goal.

—**Bell Multicultural High School, November 12, 2013**

IT REMINDED ME of my dad, you know? Working
class folks that are doing jobs that aren't that fun,
but it pays the bills. So it showed me the respect I
needed to have for the folks who work every day,
and it sent me straight to college.

—**on her first job at a book-bindery, "First Lady Michelle
Obama Talks Her Firsts," *The Tonight Show*,
February 21, 2014**

I HAD PARENTS who told me, 'Don't worry about what other people say about you.' I worked really hard. I did focus on school. I wanted an A. I wanted to be smart.

—"'Michelle: Her First Year as First Lady' excerpt: The mom-in-chief effect," *The Washington Post*, January 17, 2010

MY WHOLE IDENTITY was bound up in checking those boxes, winning every award I could, and I was good at it too. By the time I got to my high school graduation, I was at the top of my class, member of the National Honor Society, student class treasurer, and my college dream had come true—I was heading to Princeton that fall.

—commencement address at Martin Luther King, Jr. Magnet High School, May 18, 2013

I HAVE FOUND that at Princeton no matter how liberal and open-minded some of my white professors and classmates try to be toward me, I sometimes feel like a visitor on campus; as if I really don't belong.

—**"Michelle Obama's Career Timeout,"** *The Washington Post*, **May 11, 2007**

I TRIED TO recreate a community of comfort for myself and I did that by pretty much staying very close to the Black community that was there. It was a place of comfort for me in this bastion I call it. I was a poppy seed in a sea of whiteness.

—**on finding community at Princeton, "Michelle Obama Shares Her Chicago Lessons," WBEZ 91.5, November 13, 2018**

So you go in with a feeling like, 'Well I certainly can't not show up. I've gotta prove to these people that I belong here.'

—"Becoming, Part 1," *All Things Considered*, November 9, 2018

I know how it feels to be overlooked. To be underestimated. To have someone only half-listen to your ideas at a meeting.

—Let Girls Learn Event Celebrating International Women's Day, March 8, 2016

This may be the fundamental problem with caring a lot about what others think: It can put you on the established path—the my-isn't-that-impressive path—and keep you there for a long time. Maybe it stops you from swerving, from ever even considering a swerve, because what you risk losing in terms of other people's high regard can feel too costly.

—*Becoming*, p. 91, November 2018

I NARROWED MYSELF to being this thing I thought I should be. It took loss—losses in my life that made me think, 'Have you ever stopped to think about who you wanted to be?' And I realized I had not.

—*O, The Oprah Magazine,* **December 2018**

LOSING MY DAD exacerbated my sense that there was no time to sit around and ponder how my life should go. . . . If I died, I didn't want people remembering me for the stacks of legal briefs I'd written or the corporate trademarks I'd helped defend. I felt certain that I had something more to offer the world. It was time to make a move.

—*Becoming,* **p. 146, November 2018**

The ability to read, write, and analyze. The confidence to stand up and demand justice and equality. The qualifications and connections to get your foot in that door and take your seat at the table. All of that starts with education.

—Let Girls Learn Event Celebrating International Women's Day, March 8, 2016

PUBLIC ALLIES WAS all about promise—finding it, nurturing it, and putting it to use. It was a mandate to seek out young people whose best qualities might otherwise be overlooked and to give them a chance to do something meaningful. To me, the job felt almost like destiny.

>   —on working for Public Allies, an organization that helps people enter careers in public service and nonprofit work, *Becoming*, p. 176, November 2018

I DIDN'T GROW up with a lot of money. I never even imagined being the First Lady of the United States. But because I had an education, when the time came to do this, I was ready.

>   —"First Lady's Dance Moves Woo Indian Crowds," *The New York Times*, November 8, 2010

Marriage

IF MY UPS and downs, our ups and downs in our marriage can help young couples sort of realize that good marriages take work ... It's unfair to the institution of marriage, and it's unfair for young people who are trying to build something, to project this perfection that doesn't exist.

—"The Obamas' Marriage," *The New York Times,*
October 26, 2009

MARRIAGE IS A choice you make every day. It can be hard work, but when two people commit to seeing that work through, the rewards are as sweet as they come.

—Twitter, May 21, 2020

THIS IS ONE of the things I love about Barack.... He grew up with a single mom, his grandmother was the true head of household, he married me, he's got Malia and Sasha, who do not mince their words, and he has sustained himself through a life of strong women.

—"Michelle Obama on Keeping Marriage, Politics Separate," ABC News, October 8, 2012

BEFORE I MET Barack, I was all about checking off the next box—law school, law firm, nice car. But he taught me the art of the swerve, how to take life as it comes and follow your passions wherever they lead.

—*O, The Oprah Magazine*, April 15, 2020

AND MEETING BARACK Obama and falling in love with him and having somebody in your life that you cared about that influenced you and encouraged you to take some risks helped me begin to start my swerve and to leave the law and start going into public service and working for the government.

—"Michelle Obama Shares Her Chicago Lessons," WBEZ 91.5, November 13, 2018

IT WAS SORT of a bone of contention, because I was, like, 'Look, buddy, I'm not one of these who'll just hang out forever.' You know, that's just not who I am. He was, like 'Marriage, it doesn't mean anything, it's really how you feel.' And I was, like, 'Yeah, right.'

—"The Other Obama," *The New Yorker*, March 2, 2008

OUR LIFE BEFORE moving to Washington was filled with simple joys. Saturdays at soccer games, Sundays at grandma's house. And a date night for Barack and me was either dinner or a movie, because as an exhausted mom, I couldn't stay awake for both.

—Democratic National Convention, September 4, 2012

THE STRENGTHS AND challenges of our marriage don't change because we move to a different address.

—"The Obamas' Marriage," *The New York Times*, October 26, 2009

BUT WE DIDN'T always live in the White House. And for many years before coming to Washington, I was a working mother, doing my best to juggle the demands of my job with the needs of my family, with a husband who has crazy ideas.

—"Michelle Obama's remarks at Workplace Flexibility Conference," *The Washington Post*, March 31, 2010

MARRIAGE IS HARD, and raising a family together is a hard thing. It takes a toll. But if you're with the person, if you know why you're with them, if you understand that there is a friendship and a foundation there, it may feel like it goes away during those hard times, but it's something that we always come back to.

—"Oprah's 2020 Vision Tour Visionaries: Michelle Obama Interview," February 12, 2020

[BARACK] GREW UP without his mother in his life for most of his years, and he knew his mother loved him dearly, right? I always thought love was up close. Love is the dinner table, love is consistency, it is presence. So I had to share my vulnerability and also learn to love differently.

—*O, The Oprah Magazine*, December 2018

I AM LIKE a lit match. It's like, poof! And he wants to rationalize everything. So he had to learn how to give me, like, a couple minutes—or an hour—before he should even come in the room when he's made me mad. And he has to understand that he can't convince me out of my anger.

—*O, The Oprah Magazine*, December 2018

I WAS ONE of those wives who thought, 'I'm taking you to marriage counseling, so you can be fixed, Barack Obama.' Because I was like, 'I'm perfect.' But marriage counseling was a turning point for me, understanding that it wasn't up to my husband to make me happy. That I had to learn how to fill myself up, and have to put myself higher on my priority list.

—"Michelle Obama Gets Real on Marriage Counseling, Saying 'Bye, Felicia' to the Presidency," *The Tonight Show*, December 18, 2018

I'VE HAD TO come to the point of figuring out how to carve out what kind of life I want for myself beyond who Barack is and what he wants.

—"The Obamas' Marriage," *The New York Times*,
October 26, 2009

IT'S JUST ME and [Barack] and Bo and Sunny at dinner, and they don't talk—the dogs don't—so we're looking at each other.

—"Oprah's 2020 Vision Tour Visionaries: Michelle
Obama Interview," February 12, 2020

[BARACK'S] A COMPETITOR. He's an athlete. Even playing a pick-up game, even playing Scrabble, he likes to win.

—"A Political Phenomenon," *60 Minutes*,
December 25, 2008

We are happy people, but why wouldn't we be? We have our health. We have each other. We have a sense of purpose.

—"Oprah and Michelle Obama: Your Life in Focus,"
Oprah's SuperSoul Conversations, February 12, 2020

[BARACK] DOESN'T UNDERSTAND fashion. He's always asking, 'Is that new? I haven't seen that before.' It's like: 'Why don't you mind your own business? Solve world hunger. Get out of my closet.'

—**"Wrapped in Their Identities,"** *The New York Times*,
December 24, 2009

[THE PRESIDENCY] HAS definitely brought us closer. It wasn't until we moved to the White House that we were together seven days a week, that we could have dinner together, that he had time to coach the girls' teams, and go to all the events.

—**"The Final Interview With The Obamas (Full Interview)," PeopleTV, December 20, 2016**

ONE OF THE reasons I fell in love with you [Barack] is because you're guided by the principle that we are each other's brother's and sister's keepers, and that's how I was raised.

—**"President Barack Obama,"** *The Michelle Obama Podcast,* **July 29, 2020**

WE WENT THROUGH a tough time, we did some hard things together, and now we're out on the other end.

—**"Oprah and Michelle Obama: Your Life in Focus,"** *Oprah's SuperSoul Conversations*, **February 12, 2020**

I CAN LOOK at him [Barack] and I still recognize my husband. He's still the man that I fell in love with, who I value and I respect and I trust. He's been an amazing father through so much. He has shown up well in the world. He has been who he promised he would be to me.

—**"Oprah's 2020 Vision Tour Visionaries: Michelle Obama Interview," February 12, 2020**

Parenting

KIDS WILL MODEL what they see at home, and the values that are promoted at home, so whether they have a lot or a little, they still know what their parents believe and what they expect.

> —"Meet the Author: Michelle Obama," Virgin,
> December 11, 2018

ONE RULE IS: keep mom happy.

> —commencement address at Tuskegee University,
> May 12, 2015

BARACK AND I were both raised by families who didn't have much in the way of money or material possessions, but who had given us something far more valuable: their unconditional love. Their unflinching sacrifice. And a chance to go places they had never imagined for themselves.

> —Democratic National Convention, September 4, 2012

First of all, you gotta have a mate that shares your values. . . . Parenting is a verb. It is an active, engaging thing.

—"Oprah's 2020 Vision Tour Visionaries: Michelle Obama Interview," February 12, 2020

I GIVE [MALIA and Sasha] so much advice. They're so sick of me.

—"Oprah's 2020 Vision Tour Visionaries: Michelle Obama Interview," February 12, 2020

IF BARACK IS in the White House or in our house, the girls are going to be the center of our universe. We're going to make sure they're protected and that they have some level of normalcy.

—"American Girls: For Obama's daughters, White House life isn't going to be normal," *The Chicago Tribune*, November 7, 2008

[THE CHILDREN] GREW up with such odd circumstances. Campaign events and people cheering and ice cream all the time. You're trying to keep them balanced, so a lot of what we did is pretend like, 'This is normal, this is fine.' And keep them on a straight and clear path.

—*The Late Show with Stephen Colbert*, December 1, 2018

WE HAD TO parent by creating this cocoon of normalcy in a pretty crazy abnormal world.

—*Conan O'Brien Needs A Friend,* **March 17, 2019**

I'M GOING TO try to take them to school every morning—as much as I can. . . . I like to be a presence in my kids' school. I want to know the teacher; I want to know the other parents.

—**"Michelle Obama to Grace Cover of *Vogue* Magazine,"**
The Washington Post, February 10, 2009

EVERY OTHER MONTH [since] I've had children I've struggled with the notion of 'Am I being a good parent? Can I stay home? Should I stay home? How do I balance it all?' I have gone back and forth every year about whether I should work.

—**"Michelle Obama's Career Timeout," *The Washington***
***Post,* May 11, 2007**

I AM IN awe of my children for the way they have managed this whole thing with poise and grace. There's a resilience that they've had to develop.

—*Conan O'Brien Needs A Friend*, **March 17, 2019**

MOTHERHOOD HAS ALSO taught me that my job is not to bulldoze a path for them in an effort to eliminate all possible adversity. But instead, I need to be a safe and consistent place for them to land when they inevitably fail; and to show them, again and again, how to get up on their own.

—*Vogue*, **July 29, 2019**

WHAT I TELL my kids is, 'All I can do is give you the information. All I can do is model those choices. And all I can do is help you understand the consequences of your choices, and then I've gotta be with you as you make those choices and give you some feedback.'

—**"First Lady: Nation's Health 'Starts With Our Kids',"** *Talk of the Nation*, **June 12, 2012**

TRUTHFULLY, WE'RE BORING. We have a teenager at home, and she makes us feel inadequate every day.

—*The Jimmy Kimmel Show*, November 16, 2018

[ADOLESCENCE IS] THE period of our lives when we're finding our own voices and for the first time making independent decisions that help us figure out the person we'll become. That's why those years can be confusing and exhilarating and devastating, all at once.

—*Good Housekeeping*, December 3, 2018

SO OUR COMFORT level with our sexual health is directly tied to our, in my view, our physical overall wellbeing. And I don't want my daughters to think that they can't ask questions when something is wrong.

—"What Your Mother Never Told You About Health with Dr. Sharon Malone," *The Michelle Obama Podcast*, August 12, 2020

NOW I'M AT the stage where my kids are introducing me to music and they're like 'You don't want to hear this, Mom. The language is too bad.' I'm like, 'What are you doing listening to it, then?'

—**"The First Daughters Shield Michelle Obama from Music with Bad Language,"** *The Tonight Show*, **April 3, 2015**

BEING MOM-IN-CHIEF IS and always will be job number one.

—**commencement address at Tuskegee University, May 12, 2015**

WHAT I AM saying is that parenting takes up a lot of emotional space, and, you know, my husband was busy being president, so I don't think he understood how much time and energy … I put a lot of time and energy into parenting these girls in the White House, because we were trying to make their lives normal.

—**"Oprah's 2020 Vision Tour Visionaries: Michelle Obama Interview," February 12, 2020**

MANY WOMEN GET up before dawn to get a workout in or to savor a few minutes of alone time before the kids wake up. And I want to give all those women a big hug and let them know that there are millions of women like me who've been through it—and we've got your backs.

—*Good Housekeeping*, December 3, 2018

[MY MOM] LAID out the blueprint for how I have raised my own girls.

—Instagram, May 8, 2020

THERE ARE MANY different approaches that we try to use normalizing [Sasha and Malia's] experience. Setting the same set of expectations for our children that our parents had for us. You know, contributing around the house. Not taking your advantages for granted.

—"Meet the Author: Michelle Obama," Virgin, December 11, 2018

HAVING [SASHA AND Malia] in schools where some kind of mandatory community service was a part of the curriculum has always been important to me.

—"Meet the Author: Michelle Obama," Virgin, December 11, 2018

MALIA, FOR HER gap year, spent three months in the Amazon camping. I didn't want her to do that, but I thought what an important lesson in resilience for her, just physically, to know that she could endure something that hard and be away from home in a different country, learning a different language. So I had to have the courage to let her do that, even though I desperately wanted her to just be close to home.

—"Meet the Author: Michelle Obama," Virgin, December 11, 2018

I FEEL SO blessed and so content. I have what any parent would want. I've got a husband who loves me, I've got two kids that are healthy and happy and I wouldn't dare ask for anything more.

—"Behind-the-Scenes," ABC News, October 8, 2012

Friendships & Community

I'LL QUIT ON myself faster than I'll quit on my friends.

—**"What Your Mother Never Told You About Health with Dr. Sharon Malone,"** *The Michelle Obama Podcast*, **August 12, 2020**

I'M A PEOPLE person, so being with good friends is always a salve for me. In the White House, one of the best things I could do for myself was to invite a friend over just to talk.

—*Good Housekeeping*, **December 3, 2018**

I THINK WE underestimate the desire for people to feel a connection to each other. We take that for granted.

—**"Oprah's 2020 Vision Tour Visionaries: Michelle Obama Interview,"** **February 12, 2020**

WE GRAVITATE TO one another when we see the best and the worst in ourselves, because it makes us feel human.

—**"Oprah's 2020 Vision Tour Visionaries: Michelle Obama Interview," February 12, 2020**

I LOVE CASUAL conversations with people. . . . I love also what you learn standing in a grocery store line and overhearing someone's conversation, you know, watching their interactions with their loved one, and not being the watchee but watching, and taking that in, and understanding life and the observations that come.

—*Conan O'Brien Needs A Friend,* **March 17, 2019**

EVEN IN HARD times, our stories help cement our values and strengthen our connections. Sharing them shows us the way forward.

—**Instagram, April 27, 2020**

WE ARE ALWAYS stronger together.

—**Democratic National Convention, July 25, 2016**

THE CURRENT CLIMATE speaks down to people. We think that people don't want to talk about books and talk about deep things, and, you know, really be self-reflective.

—**"Oprah's 2020 Vision Tour Visionaries: Michelle Obama Interview," February 12, 2020**

WHEN WE PULL ourselves out of the lowest emotional depths and we channel our frustrations into studying and organizing and banding together, then we can build ourselves and our communities up. We can take on those deep-rooted problems and together. . . together we can overcome anything that stands in our way.

—**commencement address at Tuskegee University, May 12, 2015**

WHY DID I leave corporate law and go into community service? The truth is, it was selfish. I was happier. When I left that firm and started working in the city and getting out into the broader community of Chicago and seeing the interconnectedness of these neighborhoods, but being alive in the dirt and the grit of helping people, I never looked back.

—"President Barack Obama," *The Michelle Obama Podcast*, July 29, 2020

A GROUP OF good girlfriends provides a lifeline that is unlike any other.

—"The Gift of Girlfriends with Danielle, Sharon, and Kelly," *The Michelle Obama Podcast*, August 26, 2020

[MUSIC] IS MY best de-stresser in life. The times when Barack and I are at our most relaxed are when we invite some friends over who we have known forever. And you put a little music on top of that? Some good food? It renews your spirit to get back in the game.

—*Vogue*, November 11, 2016

Empathy. That's something I've been thinking a lot about lately.... If we see someone suffering or struggling, we don't stand in judgement, we reach out. Because 'there but for the grace of God, go I.' It's not a hard concept to grasp.

—Democratic National Convention,
August 17, 2020

WE CAN'T SHOW up for the world if we don't take care of ourselves first.

—Instagram, August 10, 2020

NO MATTER HOW you've grown up, no matter how you define family, all of you have someone in your life who believed in you and pushed you.

—graduation banquet speech at West Point,
May 23, 2011

WHENEVER I HAVE moments of fear or anxiety, I try to find ways to connect with others. I might call someone who I know is struggling and just let them know that I'm thinking of them. That simple act of reaching out lifts my spirits, too.

—O, The Oprah Magazine, April 15, 2020

IT IS NOT enough that I succeed on my own. I have to care about what happens to the kid in the desk next to me at school, because he's just as smart, but his mom works. And my father always taught us to take in everybody's full story, not to judge people.

—**"President Barack Obama,"** *The Michelle Obama Podcast,* July 29, 2020

THE PROBLEM IS, we don't know each other, we don't let each other in. And I said in [*Becoming*], it is hard to hate up close. It is easier to hate when you are hating a person through a filter.

—*The Late Show with Stephen Colbert,* December 1, 2018

MY SPIRIT IS lifted when I am feeling healthy, when I am surrounded by good people, you know. So I reach out to my family and to my friends. Even in this time of quarantine, I've fought to continue to find a way to stay connected to the people in my life who bring me joy.

—**"Protests and the Pandemic with Michele Norris,"** *The Michelle Obama Podcast,* August 5, 2020

IN AN UNCERTAIN world, time-tested values like honesty and integrity, empathy and compassion, that's the only real currency in life. Treating people right will never, ever fail you.

—"Dear Class of 2020" Commencement Address,
June 7, 2020

Life

Lessons

IF I COULD tell my younger self one thing, it would be to slow down and take a breath—you've got this.

—Instagram, February 12, 2020

I HAVE LEARNED that as long as I hold fast to my beliefs and values and follow my own moral compass, then the only expectations I need to live up to are my own.

—commencement address at Tuskegee University, May 12, 2015

AS A CHILD, my first doll was Malibu Barbie. That was the standard for perfection. That was what the world told me to aspire to. But then I discovered Maya Angelou, and her words lifted me right out of my own little head.

—Maya Angelou's Eulogy, June 7, 2014

WOMEN OF COLOR know how to get things done for our families, our communities, and our country. When we use our voices, people listen. When we lead, people follow. And when we do it together, there's no telling what we can accomplish.

—**Instagram, September 11, 2018**

WHEN I ENCOUNTERED doubters, when people told me I wasn't going to cut it, I didn't let that stop me—in fact, I did the opposite. I used that negativity to fuel me, to keep me going.

—**Bell Multicultural High School, November 12, 2013**

I WAKE UP every morning wondering how on the earth I am going to pull off that next minor miracle of getting through the day.

—**"Michelle Obama Adds New Role to Balancing Act,"**
The New York Times, **May 18, 2007**

THAT'S ALL LIFE is, is a bunch of stuff going wrong.

—on her miscarriage and other topics in her memoir, "Best of: Becoming Michelle Obama," *2 Dope Queens*, March 12, 2019

I DON'T KNOW about you, but as a mother, wife, professional, campaign wife, whatever it is that's on my plate, I'm drowning. . . . People told me, 'You can do it all. Just stay the course, get your education and you can raise a child, stay thin, be in shape, love your man, look good and raise healthy children.' That was a lie.

—"It's all about priorities for Michelle Obama," *The Los Angeles Times*, August 22, 2007

WHAT WE OFTEN see as a weakness or a failure is often a strength—or a turning point to something better.

—Instagram, December 30, 2019

I SPENT A lot of time mourning and questioning and reflecting and I thought a lot about everything my dad had done for me during his life. . . . As I grieved I came to realize that the best way for me to honor my dad's life was by how I lived my own life.

—commencement address at Virginia Tech, May 14, 2012

MY MOM HAS taught me most to be a good listener, to be patient, to use common sense. She has taught me to be open-minded. And what she still does for me today is that she will give me endless amounts of time just to talk and talk and talk and talk and all she does is listen. And sometimes that's all we need.

—The White House's Mother's Day Tea, May 9, 2013

Becoming who we are is an ongoing process, and thank God—because where's the fun in waking up one day and deciding there's nowhere left to go?

—*Vogue*, July 29, 2019

AND I THOUGHT to myself, 'If I died today, is this where I wanna be?' And it wasn't just one thing. It was a few things that made me step back and say, 'Alright, put down the boxes and the checks and now you have to do the hard work of thinking about who you want to become.'

—"Becoming, Part 1," *All Things Considered*,
November 9, 2018

THAT'S MY STORY. I embrace every aspect of who I am because, as I've said, I like my story. I like all the highs and the lows and the bumps in between.

—"Oprah's 2020 Vision Tour Visionaries: Michelle
Obama Interview," February 12, 2020

I REALIZED THAT if I wanted to keep my sanity and not let others define me, there was only one thing I could do, and that was to have faith in God's plan for me. I have to ignore all of the noise and be true to myself, and the rest would work itself out. So throughout this journey I have learned to block everything out and focus on my truth.

> —commencement address at Tuskegee University,
> May 12, 2015

I WANTED TO live my life by the principle that to whom much is given, much is expected.

> —commencement address at Martin Luther King, Jr.
> Magnet High School, May 18, 2013

JOB TITLES AND fancy awards come and go, but our lives are really made up of the little moments and connections in between.

> —*O, The Oprah Magazine*, April 15, 2020

I THINK PEOPLE can smell inauthenticity, and if you're not comfortable in your own skin, that comes across.

—"Michelle Obama on Childhood Fire Drills and Taming Barack Obama's Tardiness," *The Tonight Show*, December 19, 2018

ONE OF THE lessons that I grew up with was to always stay true to yourself and never let what somebody else says distract you from your goals. And so when I hear about negative and false attacks, I really don't invest any energy in them, because I know who I am.

—*Marie Claire*, October 22, 2008

I CONTINUE, TOO, to keep myself connected to a force that's larger and more potent than any one election, or leader, or news story—and that's optimism. For me, this is a form of faith, an antidote to fear.

—*Becoming*, p. 420, November 2018

ACT WITH BOTH your mind but also your heart.

> —**commencement address at Tuskegee University,**
> **May 12, 2015**

IT'S EASY TO lead by fear. It's easy to be divisive. It's easy to make people feel afraid. That's the easy thing, and it's also the short term thing. And for me, what I learned from my husband, what I learned in eight years at the White House is that this life, this world, our responsibility in it, is so much bigger than us.

> —**"Oprah's 2020 Vision Tour Visionaries: Michelle**
> **Obama Interview," February 12, 2020**

IF YOU SEE me giving a speech at a big thing, at a convention, what I'm thinking about as I'm walking to the podium is 'don't fall, don't trip, don't trip, don't fall.' I'm not thinking about the crowds, [I'm thinking] 'don't trip, don't be that meme. Get out of here in eight years without becoming a meme.'

> —**"Best of: Becoming Michelle Obama,"** *2 Dope Queens*,
> **March 12, 2019**

My journey has taught me that if we stay open—if we share what's important to us and listen carefully to what others share about their own lives—we find our strength, and we find our community.

—Instagram, May 4, 2020

IT TAKES COURAGE to share our stories with the world. . . . Making myself vulnerable led to some of the most meaningful connections of my life.

—**Instagram, May 15, 2020**

WE CAN'T DO this stuff, and we're not supposed to do this stuff, we weren't built to do this thing called life in a vacuum. It is much more hopeful, it is much more gratifying, much more effective to live this life as a 'we.'

—**"President Barack Obama,"** *The Michelle Obama Podcast,* **July 29, 2020**

I'M AN ORDINARY person who found herself on an extraordinary journey. In sharing my story, I hope to help create space for other stories and other voices, to widen the pathway for who belongs and why.

—*Becoming,* **p. 420–421, November 2018**

YOUR STORY IS what you have, what you will always have. It is something to own.

—*Becoming*, p. xi, November 2018

Part II

PUBLIC LIFE

There Isn't One Right Way to
Be an American

America: Its Politics & People

THERE ISN'T ONE right way to be an American. There isn't one way to make your contribution to this country.

—**Instagram, December 20, 2018**

WE ARE HERE because we believe in some simple truths, that no child's future should be limited because of the neighborhood they are born in. We believe that if you get sick in America, you should be able to see a doctor. We believe that if you work hard, you should make a decent wage and have a secure retirement.

—**"Party Stars' Last Push to Democratic Faithful,"** *The New York Times*, **November 1, 2010**

I HATE POLITICS.

—**Democratic National Convention, August 17, 2020**

I AM ONE of the handful of people living today who have seen firsthand the immense weight and awesome power of the presidency. And let me once again tell you this: the job is hard. It requires clearheaded judgement, a mastery of complex and competing issues, a devotion to facts and history, a moral compass, and an ability to listen.

—**Democratic National Convention, August 17, 2020**

BEING PRESIDENT DOESN'T change who you are, it reveals who you are.

—**Democratic National Convention, August 17, 2020**

I TRIED TO make home a safe place from the policy talk. I didn't want to be yet another person in his ear saying 'You should do this and you shouldn't do that.' I mean, everyone in the world thinks that they can coach the President of the United States.

—*The Late Show with Stephen Colbert*, **December 1, 2018**

CHILDREN BORN IN the last eight years will only know an African-American man being president of the United States. That changes the bar for all of our children, regardless of their race, their sexual orientation, their gender. It expands the scope of opportunity in their minds. And that's where change happens.

—*Parade*, August 15, 2013

WE FIRST HAD to win over Black people. Because Black people like my grandparents—they never believed this could happen. They wanted it. They wanted it for us. But their lives had told them, 'No. Never.'

—*O, The Oprah Magazine*, December 2018

MEN TALKED ABOUT the size of my butt, you know there were people who were telling me I was angry. That stuff hurts, you know? And it makes you sort of wonder, what are people seeing?

—"Oprah and Michelle Obama: Your Life in Focus," *Oprah's SuperSoul Conversations*, February 12, 2020

THE POLITICAL LIFE wasn't my first choice.

—"Michelle Obama on Keeping Marriage, Politics
Separate," ABC News, October 8, 2012

NUMBER ONE, I want the nation to remember that we do this. That this politics thing and a lot of stuff you read, it's a game, you know, and everybody's in on it. And you can't tell who believes what, but people are playing a role oftentimes.

—*Conan O'Brien Needs A Friend*, March 17, 2019

I THINK, IF I weren't married to him, I'd want him to be in [the White House], so I don't want to stand in the way of that.

—"A Political Phenomenon," *60 Minutes*,
December 25, 2008

[THE PRESIDENCY] IS a really hard job, and it is serious, and it requires a level of knowledge of history and patience and you have to be a reader, and you have to be someone who can handle stress, and you have to watch your words.

—Conan O'Brien Needs A Friend, **March 17, 2019**

THERE WERE DAYS, weeks, and months when I hated politics. And there were moments when the beauty of this country and its people so overwhelmed me that I couldn't speak.

—Becoming, **p. xi, November 2018**

WHEN I'M OFF the road, I'm going to Target to get the toilet paper, I'm standing on soccer fields, and I think there's just a level of connection that gets lost the further you get into being a candidate.

—**"The Other Obama,"** *The New Yorker*, **March 2, 2008**

You're judged in your community because you're not Black enough, and then you get out in the world, and you're too Black. And it's a careful tightwalk that we all walk as underrepresented people in the world, because people aren't used to your voice.

—"Becoming, Part 2," *All Things Considered*,
November 9, 2018

WHAT WE LEARNED is that in this country, there are decent people of all persuasions. And whether they agreed with us or not, when you were in their face, in their community, people were kind and gracious and generous. They reflected the values that I grew up with.

—*The Late Show with Stephen Colbert*, December 1, 2018

THE SERVICE, STRENGTH, and resilience of our veterans and their families is one of the great inspirations in my life.

—Instagram, November 12, 2018

IF EVER I'M feeling sorry for myself, or I'm feeling down, spending some time talking with the men and women who are the spouses of our service members that makes you understand that there is no problem that you can't handle, because they do it all with grace, and with dignity. They don't complain.

—"Michelle Obama & Dr. Jill Biden On Their Husbands' Bromance & More," *Entertainment Weekly*, December 15, 2016

IF WE DON'T know who people are inside, if we
don't trust their instincts and understand where
they're coming from, then we can't follow them,
which is why we've tried to be so open and clear
about who we are and how we think.

—"Wife Touts Obama's 'Moral Compass'," *The
Washington Post*, May 8, 2007

BY SHARING OUR stories—our little joys and
struggles—we can see what unites us.

—Instagram, March 14, 2019

IT'S LIKE YOU gotta do the baby steps.... You
don't start with the hardest, toughest issues
when you're trying to unite a group.

—"The Other Obama," *The New Yorker*, March 2, 2008

THE ABILITY TO vote freely, fairly—and safely—is
bigger than any single issue, party, or candidate.

—Twitter, May 21, 2020

THE LIFE THAT I'm talking about that most people are living has gotten progressively worse since I was a little girl.... So if you want to pretend like there was some point over the last couple of decades when your lives were easy, I want to meet you!

—"The Other Obama," *The New Yorker*, March 2, 2008

I KNOW THAT I am dealing with some form of low-grade depression, not just because of the quarantine but because of the racial strife and just seeing this administration, watching the hypocrisy of it day in and day out is dispiriting.

—"Protests and the Pandemic with Michele Norris," *The Michelle Obama Podcast*, August 5, 2020

IT DOESN'T MATTER what you or I think at this point, it's up to the voters now to figure out what kind of moral leadership do we demand in the White House? Regardless of party, regardless of race, regardless of gender, regardless of where you are, what do we want our president to look like? How do we want them to act? And if we vote for one set of behaviors, then that's obviously what we want, until we vote differently.

—*The Late Show with Stephen Colbert*, December 1, 2018

SOMETIMES TRUTH TRANSCENDS party.

—Twitter, June 18, 2018

THE PEOPLE WHO vote get to determine the direction of the country they're gonna live in and we have to live with this now, so the question is: what are we going to do next?

—*The Late Show with Stephen Colbert*, December 1, 2018

WE GROW UP with messages that tell us that there's only one way to be American—that if our skin is dark or our hips are wide, if we don't experience love in a particular way, if we speak another language or come from another country, then we don't belong. That is, until someone dares to start telling that story differently.

—*Becoming*, **p. 415, November 2018**

THESE DAYS, IT can be hard to feel grounded or hopeful—but the connections I've made with people across America and around the world remind me that empathy can truly be a lifeline.

—**Twitter, April 27, 2020**

The White House

IF YOU CAN'T run your own house, you can't run the White House.

> —"Michelle Obama: Did She or Didn't She?," *The New York Times*, August 21, 2007

IT'S IMPORTANT FOR young people, in particular our kids, kids of all backgrounds, of every race, and every socio-economic background, to feel like they have a place in the Nation's house. And to do that, you have to do things that make them comfortable as well. And if it's hip-hop dancing, well let's do it, you know? If it's a sleepover on the south lawn with the Girl Scouts, then let's do it. . . . Let's breathe some life into this house.

> —"The Final Interview With The Obamas (Full Interview)," PeopleTV, December 20, 2016

WE DIDN''T JUST show up in the White House, you know? I am Michelle from the Southside of Chicago. I grew up in a little bitty house. I got nice clothes and jewelry now, but my mother made my clothes, you know?

—**"Oprah's 2020 Vision Tour Visionaries: Michelle Obama Interview," February 12, 2020**

I REALIZED THAT our time in the White House would form the foundation for who they would become. And how well we managed this experience could truly make or break them. That is what Barack and I think about every day as we try to guide and protect our girls through the challenges of this unusual life in the spotlight.

—**Democratic National Convention, July 25, 2016**

I'LL ALWAYS BE grateful for the opportunity
that living in the White House afforded us, but
it probably won't come as a surprise to anyone
that sometimes it was a real challenge to keep up
with the pace. We'd be launching an initiative, or
crisscrossing the country for campaign events,
or visiting a community that was hurting from a
tornado or a senseless shooting—sometimes all
in a two- or three-day span.

—*Good Housekeeping*, December 3, 2018

I DON'T LOSE sleep over it, because the realities
are, you know, as a Black man, Barack can get
shot going to the gas station. You can't make
decisions based on fear and the possibility of
what might happen. We just weren't raised that
way.

—on if she worries the Presidency makes Barack a target
for violence, "A Political Phenomenon," *60 Minutes*,
December 25, 2008

THE PRESSURE WAS on everyone. We couldn't afford to make a mistake, we couldn't afford to look cavalier. We had to watch our language. And we also knew that everything we said... we thought about how it would be viewed by children, not just our children, but all of our children. We knew that we were the moral compass.

—*The Late Show with Stephen Colbert*, December 1, 2018

BARACK AND I were paying off our student loans until a very short time ago. We're lucky that he's had a couple of best-selling books.... But we didn't come from privileged backgrounds. We both know what it's like to struggle and work hard, and we're not very far removed from families who are doing everything they can to keep up with rising costs.

—*Marie Claire*, October 22, 2008

WE WANTED TO change things up here in the
White House a little bit. We wanted to open the
doors really wide to a bunch of different folks
who usually don't get access to this place. We
also wanted to highlight all different kinds of
American art—all the art forms: paintings, music,
culture—especially art forms that had never been
seen in these walls.

—"Hamilton at the White House" workshop,
March 14, 2016

LIN-MANUEL [MIRANDA] GOT onstage in the
East Room . . . in between the big portraits
of George and Martha Washington, and he
proceeded to perform the song "Alexander
Hamilton," which, as you all know, is the opening
number of this amazing musical. And of course,
we were blown away. There are probably shots
of us sitting there with our mouths open going,
'Who is this dude? What is he up to?'

—"Hamilton at the White House" workshop,
March 14, 2016

HAMILTON IS AN amazing story that is
beautifully told. Through *Hamilton*, Lin-Manuel
[Miranda] reveals all the drama, the glory, the
heartbreak that run through our nation's history.
And he shows us that the icons in our history
books were real people with real brilliance but
also with real flaws. So really, *Hamilton* teaches
us history the way it really should be taught.

—"Hamilton at the White House" workshop,
March 14, 2016

CLEARLY BARACK'S CAREER decisions are
leading us. They're not mine; that's obvious.
I'm married to the President of the United
States. I don't have another job, and it would be
problematic in this role.

—"The Obamas' Marriage," *The New York Times*,
October 26, 2009

When you're not engaged in the day-to-day struggles that everybody feels, you slowly start losing touch. And I think it's important for the people in the White House to have a finger on the pulse.

—*Vogue*, November 11, 2016

THE TRIPS THAT we did take as a family are ones that we'll remember for the rest of our lives. They're not normal family vacations and those experiences have definitely brought us together in ways that we wouldn't have if we weren't here.

—"The Final Interview With The Obamas (Full Interview)," PeopleTV, December 20, 2016

I KNOW THAT I've always had a big commitment to my health. But in the years in the White House I found that I was more desperate to hang on to that part of myself.

—"What Your Mother Never Told You About Health with Dr. Sharon Malone," *The Michelle Obama Podcast*, August 12, 2020

THIS IS THE first time in a long time in our marriage that we've lived seven days a week in the same household with the same schedule, with the same set of rituals. That's been more of a relief for me than I would have ever imagined.

—"The Obamas' Marriage," *The New York Times*, October 26, 2009

I RARELY STEP foot in the West Wing. In fact, people are shocked when they see me there. But, I rarely walk in that office because the truth is he's got so many wonderful advisors. I don't have the expertise and the time in to be able to provide the kind of advice and guidance that he's already getting.

—"Michelle Obama on Keeping Marriage, Politics Separate," ABC News, October 8, 2012

I THINK, FOR Barack, having somebody who's like the big brother . . . in this journey, somebody that he respects and admires. It's the best decision that Barack has made as President of the United States, picking Joe and the Bidens as our partners in this journey. That's real.

—"Michelle Obama & Dr. Jill Biden On Their Husbands' Bromance & More," *Entertainment Weekly*, December 15, 2016

WHEN BARACK COMES home he's like, 'I had lunch with Joe today,' and there's real joy in the fact.

—"Michelle Obama & Dr. Jill Biden On Their Husbands' Bromance & More," *Entertainment Weekly*, December 15, 2016

YES, THE JOB carries its stresses, for sure. . . .
When you feel that burden, you really have to fall
back on the normalcy and the love of your family.
I think probably some of the best moments for
Barack were when he could come up on that
elevator, come to the second floor, sit down at the
dinner table and have no one care about anything
he does. At all. I mean, literally. Just talked over,
talked around. 'Oh, by the way, Dad. Oh yeah,
what did you do today?'

> —"The Final Interview With The Obamas (Full
> Interview)," PeopleTV, December 20, 2016

REFLECTING, I FIND, is very important. The
truth is that for the last decade, there was
no time to even really think about what just
happened to us.

> —*The Jimmy Kimmel Show*, November 16, 2018

THE FREEDOM THAT we'll get in exchange for the privileges and the luxuries, you know.... Seven and a half years, that's enough luxuriating. I can make my own grilled cheese sandwich. I can make a mean grilled cheese sandwich.

—"Carpool Karaoke," *The Late Late Show with James Corden,* July 21, 2016

WE ARE FINDING each other again. We have dinners alone and chunks of time where it's just us—what we were when we started this thing: no kids, no publicity, no nothing. Just us and our dreams.

—*People,* November 26, 2018

Role of First Lady

WHEN YOU'RE THE first of anything, the bar feels higher. You feel like you don't have room to make mistakes.

—*The Late Show with Stephen Colbert*, **December 1, 2018**

THERE IS NO handbook for incoming First Ladies of the United States. . . . It's a strange kind of sidecar to the presidency, a seat that by the time I came to it had already been occupied by more than forty-three different women, each of whom had done it in her own way.

—*Becoming*, **p. 283, November 2018**

MY GOD, WHO can sit here and say, 'I'm ready to be President and First Lady?'

—**"Michelle Obama Adds New Role to Balancing Act,"**
The New York Times, **May 18, 2007**

I HAVEN'T HAD time to solely step back and reflect yet on my role as the first African-American [First Lady]. I just want to make sure that I'm doing a good job.

> —**"Michelle Obama on Keeping Marriage, Politics Separate," ABC News, October 8, 2012**

I CARRIED A history with me, and it wasn't that of presidents or First Ladies. I'd never related to the story of John Quincy Adams the way I did to that of Sojourner Truth, or been moved by Woodrow Wilson the way I was by Harriet Tubman. The struggles of Rosa Parks and Coretta Scott King were more familiar to me than those of Eleanor Roosevelt or Mamie Eisenhower. I carried their histories, along with those of my mother and grandmothers. . . . I wanted to show up in the world in a way that honored who they were.

> —*Becoming*, **p. 365-366, November 2018**

My view on this stuff is I'm just trying to be myself, trying to be as authentic as I can be. I can't pretend to be somebody else.

—"Michelle Obama's Career Timeout," *The Washington Post*, May 11, 2007

I hate looking at myself, I hate listening to my voice, I hate watching myself on tape, because I'm constantly judging myself too just like everybody else.

—"Oprah and Michelle Obama: Your Life in Focus," *Oprah's SuperSoul Conversations*, February 12, 2020

I think I am a better First Lady when I'm Michelle than when I'm somebody else in a magazine.

—"The First Lady's First Year," *The Washington Post*, January 18, 2010

When you're First Lady, America shows itself to you in its extremes.

—*Becoming*, p. x, November 2018

I was humbled
and excited to be
First Lady, but not
for one second
did I think I'd be
sliding into some
glamorous, easy
role. Nobody who
has the words
'first' and 'Black'
attached to them
ever would.

—*Becoming*, p. 284, November 2018

ELEANOR ROOSEVELT IS one of my idols. She is probably one of the greatest first ladies that has ever lived, with her active engagement in this country and being able to shift norms in ways that are important.

—*Cooking Light*, February 6, 2015

I MAINTAINED A code for myself, though, when it came to speaking publicly about anything or anyone in the political sphere: I said only what I absolutely believed and what I absolutely felt.

—*Becoming*, p. 407, November 2018

I HAVE AN Instagram account and a Twitter account, obviously, but I have to get permission to use it. . . from my staff. They don't trust me with it.

—*The Jimmy Kimmel Show*, November 16, 2018

HOW BARACK AND I comported ourselves in the face of instability mattered. We understood that we represented the nation and were obligated to step forward and be present when there was tragedy, or hardship, or confusion. Part of our role, as we understood it, was to model reason, compassion, and consistency.

—*Becoming*, p. 343, November 2018

THERE HAD BEEN so many times in my life when I'd found myself the only woman of color—or even the only woman, period—sitting at a conference table or attending a board meeting or mingling at one VIP gathering or another. If I was the first at some of these things, I wanted to make sure that in the end I wasn't the only—that others were coming up behind me.

—*Becoming*, p. 355, November 2018

WHEN WE HOSTED an event, I wanted everyday people to show up, not just those accustomed to black-tie attire. And I wanted more kids around, because kids made everything better.

—*Becoming*, p. 310, November 2018

I VERY MUCH felt my role as a parent to the nation. It's like, I've gotta have my stuff together. This isn't the time for me to lick my wounds, because we got stuff to do here.

—on experiencing hurt during her time as First Lady, *Conan O'Brien Needs A Friend*, March 17, 2019

I NEEDED TO demonstrate to the nation that I can do the work. I work hard and I work smart, and let me just show you. And in the end I have to count on the fact that what I produce will define me. And so that's what it means to go high. In the end, don't seek revenge, don't harbor resentment. Just do the work.

—*Conan O'Brien Needs A Friend*, March 17, 2019

OF COURSE I am proud of my country. Nowhere but in America could my story be possible.

—"Michelle Obama Shows Her Warmer Side on 'The View'," *The New York Times*, June 19, 2008

I TAKE THE words that I say to children very seriously. When I am with a young person, I want them to hear me see them. It's important for them to know that this person, who's so famous and has this platform, thinks that they are beautiful and smart and kind and good. And that has meaning.

—"Oprah's 2020 Vision Tour Visionaries: Michelle Obama Interview," February 12, 2020

Let's Move! & Children's Health

RARELY IN THE history of this country have we encountered a problem of such magnitude and consequence that is so eminently solvable. So instead of just talking about this issue, or worrying and wringing our hands about it, we decided to get moving.

—American Grown: The Story of the White House Kitchen Garden and Gardens Across America, p. 178, May 2012

THIS ISN'T ABOUT inches and pounds or how our kids look. It's about how our kids feel and how they feel about themselves.

—"First Lady Michelle Obama: 'Let's move' and work on childhood obesity problem," *The Washington Post*, **February 10, 2010**

I HAVE YET to meet a single parent who doesn't understand the threat of obesity to their health and to their children's health. And they're looking for solutions.

—Let's Move! Food Marketing, September 18, 2013

I DON'T WANT our kids to live diminished lives because we failed to step up today. I don't want them looking back decades from now and asking us, 'Why didn't you help us when you had a chance? Why didn't you put us first when it mattered most?'

—**"First Lady Michelle Obama: 'Let's move' and work on childhood obesity problem,"** *The Washington Post*, **February 10, 2010**

WE UNDERESTIMATE IT, but my goal personally is that when I'm 80 and 90 years old, I want to be moving around. I want to be able to travel. I want to be able to walk up a temple or a ruin on my own and see the world. And I can only do that if I've been investing in my health now.

—*Cooking Light*, **February 6, 2015**

FROM THE BEGINNING, I knew I wanted children to play a major role in the creation and growth of our garden. I particularly wanted to include local kids who had never dreamed of visiting the White House despite living in the same city.

—*American Grown: The Story of the White House Kitchen Garden and Gardens Across America*, p. 54, May 2012

I ALSO KNEW that I wanted this new White House garden to be a 'learning garden,' a place where people could have a hands-on experience of working the soil and children who have never seen a plant sprout could put down seeds and seedlings that would take root. And I wanted them to come back for the harvest, to be able to see and taste the fruits (and vegetables) of their labors.

—*American Grown: The Story of the White House Kitchen Garden and Gardens Across America*, p. 10, May 2012

WE EVENTUALLY SETTLED on a spot at the back edge of the South Lawn that could easily be seen from outside the White House gate. That was important to me because I wanted this to be the people's garden, just as the White House is the 'people's house.' I wanted people who were just walking by to be able to share in what we were doing and growing.

—*American Grown: The Story of the White House Kitchen Garden and Gardens Across America*, **p. 31, May 2012**

IN FACT, EQUALITY is a key part of the message of planting day. We are all down in the dirt. Anyone present can help dig. There is no hierarchy, no boss, and no winner. It is almost impossible to mess up. We make it clear that gardening isn't about perfection.

—*American Grown: The Story of the White House Kitchen Garden and Gardens Across America*, **p. 54, May 2012**

Without anyone expecting it, our garden has become a community garden, connecting people from all different backgrounds, ages, and walks of life. We all share in its care and in its success; and here in this garden, each of us, in our own way, has been able to put down roots.

—*American Grown: The Story of the White House Kitchen Garden and Gardens Across America,* p. 86–87, May 2012

I'VE ALWAYS BELIEVED that kids learn the most when they're least afraid of making mistakes and they have the support they need to try, and fail, and try again.

—American Grown: The Story of the White House Kitchen Garden and Gardens Across America, p. 55, May 2012

WHEN WE ENGAGE children in harvesting our gardens—when we teach them about where their food comes from, how to prepare it, and how to grow it themselves—they reap the benefits well into the future.

—American Grown: The Story of the White House Kitchen Garden and Gardens Across America, p. 137, May 2012

I'VE HULA-HOOPED AND done push-ups on the White House lawn. I've jumped Double Dutch and run through an obstacle course of cardboard boxes carrying water jugs. I've potato-sack raced with comedian Jimmy Fallon. I've even danced 'the Dougie' to Beyoncé with a bunch of middle schoolers. But there's a method to my madness. We know that as parents, we are our kids' first and best role models, and I want kids to see that there are all kinds of ways to be active.

—*American Grown: The Story of the White House Kitchen Garden and Gardens Across America*, p. 199, May 2012

THAT'S WHAT GREAT American companies do. They act boldly, they innovate, they take risks. And remember, it wasn't that long ago that 'going green' or taking your business online were considered risky endeavors. But throughout our history, the companies that saw where the future was headed and took that leap have been rewarded.

—Let's Move! Food Marketing, September 18, 2013

WHILE OUR GOAL was ambitious, the idea behind Let's Move! was very simple: that all of us—parents and teachers; doctors and coaches; business, faith, and community leaders; and others—have a role to play in helping our kids lead healthier lives.

—*American Grown: The Story of the White House Kitchen Garden and Gardens Across America*, **p. 178, May 2012**

IT IS MY hope that our garden's story—and the stories of gardens across America—will inspire families, schools, and communities to try their own hand at gardening and enjoy all the gifts of health, discovery, and connection a garden can bring.

—*American Grown: The Story of the White House Kitchen Garden and Gardens Across America*, **p. 19, May 2012**

THOSE FIRST SEEDS we planted in our garden helped start a conversation that grew into a nationwide movement as people across this country united to address the challenge of childhood obesity. And together, with determination and creativity, we have begun building the foundation for a healthier generation and a healthier nation.

—*American Grown: The Story of the White House Kitchen Garden and Gardens Across America*, **p. 165, May 2012**

So I THOUGHT that a garden in the backyard of the White House would be a wonderful way to begin a conversation about what we feed our kids and their overall health.

—**"First Lady: Nation's Health 'Starts With Our Kids',"** *Talk of the Nation*, **June 12, 2012**

PEOPLE JUST WEREN'T able to be critical of their own children.... So we knew if we were going to tackle this issue, we would have to change the cultural perspective on the issue as a whole.

—*Variety*, August 23, 2016

THE BOTTOM LINE is very simple: As parents, we always put our children's interests first.... And when we make decisions about our kids' health, we rely on doctors and experts who can give us accurate information based on sound science. Our leaders in Washington should do the same.

—"The Campaign for Junk Food," *The New York Times*, May 28, 2014

YOU SEE PEOPLE'S struggles up close and personal. And what you see on the ground is often the first indicator of what's happening on a national level.

—"Michelle Obama talks to mayors about her initiative to combat childhood obesity," *The Washington Post*, January 21, 2010

THIS ISN'T ABOUT trying to turn the clock back to when we were kids or preparing five-course meals from scratch every night. No one has time for that. And it's not about being 100 percent perfect, 100 percent of the time. Lord knows I'm not. There's a place for cookies and ice cream, burgers and fries—that's part of the fun of childhood.

—"First Lady Michelle Obama: 'Let's move' and work on childhood obesity problem," *The Washington Post*, February 10, 2010

A LOT OF kids don't understand that food is fuel in a very fundamental way. And sometimes they don't listen to grown-ups, and they don't listen to the First Lady. But many of them will listen to you [fellow kids] because you're living proof of that reality.

—Kids' State Dinner, July 10, 2015

AT THE END of the day, if we truly want to solve this problem [of childhood obesity], we also need to get our kids to actually want to eat these healthier options. And I say this not just as a First Lady who's been working on this issue for the past three and a half years; I say this as a mom who has been working hard to raise two girls.

—**Let's Move! Food Marketing, September 18, 2013**

FROM THE TIMES our kids are still in diapers, we as parents are already fighting an uphill battle to get them interested in the foods that will actually nourish them and help them grow.

—**Let's Move! Food Marketing, September 18, 2013**

As both a mother and a First Lady, I was alarmed by reports of skyrocketing childhood obesity rates and the dire consequences for our children's health. And I hoped this garden would help begin a conversation about this issue—a conversation about the food we eat, the lives we lead, and how all of that affects our children.

—American Grown: The Story of the White House Kitchen Garden and Gardens Across America, p. 9, May 2012

In fact, whenever we invite kids to help us harvest the garden, I'm struck by their eagerness, diligence, and focus.

—American Grown: The Story of the White House Kitchen Garden and Gardens Across America, p. 123, May 2012

We don't need to wait for some new invention or discovery to make this happen. This doesn't require fancy tools or technologies. We have everything we need right now. The only question is whether we have the will.

—"Michelle Obama talks to mayors about her initiative to combat childhood obesity," *The Washington Post*, January 21, 2010

AT THE WHITE House Kitchen Garden, we want kids to witness the entire journey of their food, from soil to table. So at our very first fall harvest, we invited them into the White House kitchen, where they helped cook a meal of grilled chicken, salad, brown rice, peas, and honey cupcakes. We didn't know whether the kids would like the vegetables, but they devoured the salad and asked for more.

—*American Grown: The Story of the White House Kitchen Garden and Gardens Across America*, **p. 125, May 2012**

WHETHER IT'S A few plants in the backyard or on the windowsill, a small garden near the town center, or a vast tract of land with crops as far as the eye can see, year after year, season after season, gardens bring individuals and communities together.

—*American Grown: The Story of the White House Kitchen Garden and Gardens Across America*, **p. 213, May 2012**

WE ALSO KNOW that we need to attack this problem from every angle, because we can serve kids the healthiest school lunches imaginable, but if there's no supermarket in their community, and they don't have nutritious food at home, then they still won't have a healthy diet. We can build shiny new supermarkets on every block, but if parents don't have the information they need, they'll still struggle to make healthy choices for their kids. And if kids aren't active, then no matter how well we feed them, they still won't be leading healthy lives.

—American Grown: The Story of the White House Kitchen Garden and Gardens Across America, **p. 178–180, May 2012**

I WANTED TO make sure that it was a teaching garden. So we worked with kids in local schools who come and help us do everything from digging up the soil, to doing the first planting, to harvesting, to eating the bounty.

—**"First Lady: Nation's Health 'Starts With Our Kids',"** *Talk of the Nation,* **June 12, 2012**

I KNOW THAT many other parents have had a similar experience. We want to buy healthy food, but it can sometimes be hard to find—and afford—products that are good for our kids and taste good too. That's why through Let's Move!, we're working with businesses and organizations across America to give parents the information and opportunities they need to make healthier choices for their families.

—American Grown: The Story of the White House Kitchen Garden and Gardens Across America, p. 182, **May 2012**

IT'S A SOCIAL justice issue. Every child in this country, every person in this country, should have access to good food.

—"First Lady Michelle Obama: 'Let's move' and work on childhood obesity problem," *The Washington Post*, **February 10, 2010**

Part III

WORLDVIEW

A Better World is Always Possible

Making

Change

A FAIRER, MORE just, and more loving world is always possible.

—**Twitter, June 26, 2020**

WE WANT OUR children—and all children in this nation—to know that the only limit to the height of your achievements is the reach of your dreams and your willingness to work for them.

—**Democratic National Convention, August 25, 2008**

NO MATTER WHAT kind of life you want to build for yourself, you've already got the raw materials inside.

—**Instagram, September 18, 2018**

TO ANYONE OUT there who feels like the world is stacked against them, know that I'm rooting for you to succeed and reach your full potential.

—**Instagram, July 23, 2019**

ONE THING I know is that it's up to us to be
there for each other—especially those who
often feel overlooked—because when someone
shows genuine interest in your growth and
development, it can make all the difference in the
world.

—Instagram, March 6, 2019

THINGS GET BETTER when regular folks take
action to make change happen from the bottom
up. Every major historical moment in our time,
it has been made by folks who said, 'Enough,'
and they banded together to move this country
forward—and now is one of those times.

—**"Michelle Obama's family tree has roots in a Carolina
slave plantation,"** *The Chicago Tribune*,
December 1, 2008

THIS IS HOW you can finish the work that the
generations before you started. By staying open
and hopeful, even through tough times. Even
through discomfort and pain.

—**Twitter, June 7, 2020**

I BELIEVE THAT each of us—no matter what our age or background or walk of life—each of us has something to contribute to the life of this nation.

—**Democratic National Convention, August 25, 2008**

TALENT AND AMBITION know no distinctions of race, nationality, wealth, or fame.

—**commencement address at City College of New York, June 3, 2016**

ANGER IS A powerful force. It can be a useful force, but left on its own, it will only corrode and destroy and sow chaos on the inside and out. But when anger is focused, when it's channeled into something more, that is the stuff that changes history.

—**"Dear Class of 2020" Commencement Address, June 7, 2020**

THE FIRST STEP in making lasting change is understanding the best, most effective routes to achieve it.

—Instagram, June 13, 2020

I HAVE NEVER been afraid to be a little silly, and you can engage people that way. My view is, first you get them to laugh, then you get them to listen. So I'm always game for a good joke.

—*Variety*, August 23, 2016

WE CANNOT ALLOW our hurt and our frustration to turn us against each other, to cancel somebody else's point of view if we don't agree with every last bit of their approach. That kind of thinking only divides us and distracts us from our higher calling. It is the gum in the wheel of progress.

—"Dear Class of 2020" Commencement Address,
June 7, 2020

TALENT AND EFFORT, combined with our various backgrounds and life experiences, has always been the lifeblood of our singular American genius.

—commencement address at City College of New York, June 3, 2016

WHEN SOMETHING DOESN'T go your way, you've just got to adjust. You've got to dig deep and work like crazy. And that's when you'll find out what you're really made of.

—commencement address at Martin Luther King, Jr. Magnet High School, May 18, 2013

YOUR GREATEST ACHEIVEMENTS will never come easily, and they will never be achieved alone.

—graduation banquet speech at West Point, May 23, 2011

I THINK IT is so easy, and lazy, to lead by fear. It is much harder to lead with hope.

—*The Late Show with Stephen Colbert*, December 1, 2018

MY PURPOSE ON this planet is not to just take care of my own little ego. There is a bigger purpose for me out there. So, when I respond to something, I have to think about that light I'm trying to shine. What role model am I trying to be?

—"Oprah's 2020 Vision Tour Visionaries: Michelle Obama Interview," February 12, 2020

THROUGH SERVICE, WE can heal ourselves.

—commencement address at Virginia Tech, May 14, 2012

OUR GREATNESS COMES when we appreciate each others' strengths, when we learn from each other, when we lean on each other.

—commencement address at City College of New York, June 3, 2016

Make a decision to use your privilege and your voice for the things that really matter. . . . Share that voice with the rest of the world. For those of you that feel invisible, please know that your story matters. Your ideas matter. Your experiences matter. Your vision for what the world can and should be matters.

—"Dear Class of 2020" Commencement Address,
June 7, 2020

CAUSE I DON'T want you to think that when you have a problem you're broken. I think that, that's the message. If I'm perfect, then when you're not, which is inevitable, you think you're failing. And it's like no, you're just living life.

—**"Best of: Becoming Michelle Obama,"** *2 Dope Queens*,
March 12, 2019

YOUR STORY MATTERS—but if you don't see that, chances are no one else will either.

—**Instagram, February 25, 2019**

NO MATTER WHAT path you choose, I want you to make sure it's you choosing it and not someone else.

—**commencement address at Tuskegee University,**
May 12, 2015

IF IT'S NOT gonna fix a problem, if it's not gonna move the needle, then you're not going high— you're just being selfish.

—**"Oprah and Michelle Obama: Your Life in Focus,"** ***Oprah's SuperSoul Conversations*, February 12, 2020**

REMEMBER TO ALWAYS stay open to new experiences and never let the doubters get in the way.

—**Instagram, December 19, 2018**

ALL OF US are driven by a simple belief that the world as it is just won't do—that we have an obligation to fight for the world as it should be.

—**Democratic National Convention, August 25, 2008**

HISTORY IS MADE by the people who show up for the fight, even when they know they might not be fully recognized for their contributions.

—***Harper's Bazaar*, June 22, 2020**

FOR SO MANY people, TV and movies may be the only way they understand people who aren't like them. It becomes important for the world to see different images of each other, so that we can develop empathy and understanding.

—*Variety*, August 23, 2016

IT'S NOT WHO'S in the White House. It's not who is the First Lady. You can give a lift, but once you give people that information, and help them understand that they have the power to make the change, then change actually happens.

—*Variety*, August 23, 2016

AS MOTHERS, SISTERS, friends, and mentors, we all have a role to play in helping our boys and young men of color fulfill their boundless potential.

—Twitter, February 22, 2019

I HATE WHEN people who are in the public eye and even seek the public eye say, 'Well, I'm not a role model because I don't want that responsibility.' Too late. You are.... And I don't want young people to look at me here and now as Michelle Obama and think, 'Well, she never had it rough. She never had challenges; she never had fears.'

—*O, The Oprah Magazine*, December 2018

I'M HAPPY TO share my story, if it helps.

—"**Michelle Obama says her brother is still their mother's favorite,**" *Good Morning America*, **November 13, 2018**

TOO OFTEN, WE focus on what I call our 'stats.' What school did you go to? What's your occupation? But the truth is, to really get to know people, we have to go deep into those stories. I felt that if I wanted people to get to know me, I had to share everything.... And that's really the way I live my life.

—"Meet the Author: Michelle Obama," Virgin, December 11, 2018

I RECOGNIZE NOW that the memoir and the tour were really different than what I'd done before—I wasn't promoting a policy or rallying votes; I was out there, alone, talking about my feelings and vulnerabilities.

—*People*, December 4, 2019

I AM MAKING my mark in hopes that my grandchildren will experience something better than I did, just as my parents laid down markers so that my life would be better than theirs. We don't fix things in a lifetime.

—"Becoming, Part 2," *All Things Considered,*
November 9, 2018

Inequality

&

Injustice

EVEN THOUGH THE story has never been tidy, and Black folks have had to march and fight for every inch of our freedom, our story is nonetheless one of progress.

—**Instagram, June 19, 2020**

IF WE WANT to keep making progress on issues like racial justice, we've got to be willing to start hard conversations—especially with the people we love.

—**Instagram, July 27, 2020**

MY EXPERIENCES AT Princeton have made me far more aware of my 'Blackness' than ever before. Regardless of the circumstances under which I interact with whites at Princeton, it often seems as if, to them, I will always be Black first and a student second.

—**"Michelle, Meritocracy and Me,"** *The Washington Post*, **July 20, 2008**

THERE WILL ALWAYS be folks who make assumptions about you based on superficial things like where you're from or what you're wearing or how you look. There will always be folks who judge you based on just one thing that you say or do, folks who define you based on one isolated incident.

—commencement address at Virginia Tech,
May 14, 2012

WHEN I'M JUST a Black woman, I've noticed that white people don't even see me. They're not even looking at me.

—"The Gift of Girlfriends with Danielle, Sharon, and Kelly," *The Michelle Obama Podcast*, August 26, 2020

I REMEMBERED THEM all, every person who'd ever waved me forward, doing his or her best to inoculate me against the slights and indignities I was certain to encounter in the places I was headed—all those environments built primarily for and by people who were neither Black nor female.

—*Becoming*, p. 355, November 2018

WE HAD HAD incidents of going into the suburbs—Park Forest—that were all white and I write about the incident where somebody scratched my father's car because we were Black folks in a neighborhood.

—"President Barack Obama," *The Michelle Obama Podcast*, July 29, 2020

THERE'S AN AGE-OLD maxim in the Black community: You've got to be twice as good to get half as far. As the first African American family in the White House, we were being viewed as representatives of our race. Any error or lapse in judgment, we knew, would be magnified, read as something more than what it was.

—*Becoming*, p. 295, November 2018

WAKING UP TO yet another story of a Black man or a Black person somehow being dehumanized or hurt or killed or falsely accused of something, it is exhausting. And it has led to a weight that I haven't felt in my life in a while.

—"Protests and the Pandemic with Michele Norris," *The Michelle Obama Podcast*, August 5, 2020

Going high does not mean putting on a smile and saying nice things when confronted by viciousness and cruelty. Going high means taking the harder path, means scraping and clawing our way to the mountaintop. Going high means standing fierce against hatred.

–Democratic National Convention,
August 17, 2020

ALL THESE KIDS wouldn't be out in the streets if they weren't hearing something that made the sight of these killings or the knowledge of these killings intolerable to them where they are taking to the streets at the expense of their health in the middle of a pandemic. That is powerful.

—**"Protests and the Pandemic with Michele Norris,"** *The Michelle Obama Podcast*, **August 5, 2020**

WHEN IT COMES to all those tidy stories of hard work and self-determination that we like to tell ourselves about America, well, the reality is a lot more complicated than that. Because for too many people in this country, no matter how hard they work, there are structural barriers working against them that just make the road longer and rockier.

—**"Dear Class of 2020" Commencement Address, June 7, 2020**

IT IS NOT your circumstance that defines your future—it's your attitude.... You decide how you're going to respond when something doesn't go your way.

—**Bell Multicultural High School, November 12, 2013**

AS FIRST LADY, I had the opportunity to meet with kids living in underserved communities— kids fighting every day just to stay alive. And what I saw in those kids was as much grit, and heart, and promise as any child growing up in wealthier areas. That's something I hope more folks recognize—that kids growing up in tougher environments have skills and experiences that a lot of their peers just can't compete with.

—*The National*, **Amtrak, August/September 2019**

If we ever hope to move past [racism], it can't just be on people of color to deal with it. It's up to all of us—Black, white, everyone— no matter how well-meaning we think we might be, to do the honest, uncomfortable work of rooting it out.

—Instagram, May 29, 2020

THAT IS THE story of this country.... The story of generations of people who felt the lash of bondage, the shame of servitude, the sting of segregation, but who kept on striving and hoping and doing what needed to be done, so that today, I wake up every morning in a house that was built by slaves. And I watch my daughters, two beautiful, intelligent, Black young women, playing with their dogs on the White House lawn.

—**Democratic National Convention, July 25, 2016**

ALTHOUGH, THERE HAVE been periods throughout this quarantine where I just have felt too low. You know, I've gone through those emotional highs and lows that I think everybody feels, where you just don't feel yourself.

—**"Protests and the Pandemic with Michele Norris,"** *The Michelle Obama Podcast*, **August 5, 2020**

WHAT TRULY MAKES our country great is its diversity. I've seen that beauty in so many ways over the years. Whether we are born here or seek refuge here, there's a place for us all. We must remember it's not my America or your America. It's our America.

—Twitter, June 19, 2019

Supporting Women & Girls

WE KNOW THAT when we give girls a chance to learn, they'll seize it. And when they do, our whole world benefits.

—**Instagram, September 5, 2019**

IF WE WANT our daughters to dream big, we as women have to dig way down deep and figure out what fights are worth it for our kids.

—**Instagram, May 5, 2018**

IT'S UP TO us, as mothers and mother-figures, to give the girls in our lives the kind of support that keeps their flame lit and lifts up their voices—not necessarily with our own words, but by letting them find the words themselves.

—*People*, **May 27, 2019**

WHEN I GET up and work out, I'm working out just as much for my girls as I am for me, because I want them to see a mother who loves them dearly, who invests in them, but who also invests in herself. It's just as much about letting them know as young women that it is okay to put yourself a little higher on your priority list.

—*Prevention Magazine*, **March 2012**

RAISING STRONG GIRLS isn't just about what we do as women—it's about the example the men in their lives set, too.

—**Twitter, June 16, 2019**

[MY PARENTS] DIDN'T expect the same thing from me as they did from my brother, but they did treat us as equals, which I think played a big role in me being a powerful woman with a powerful voice. I was used to being respected in my home, so I went out into the world and I expected that same treatment from others.

—**"Meet the Author: Michelle Obama," Virgin, December 11, 2018**

I WANT TO make sure that men understand the importance of male role models in the life of a strong girl.

> —"Michelle Obama says her brother is still their mother's favorite," *Good Morning America*, November 13, 2018

FOR A GIRL to have strong men in her life, like I had, a father who loved me, a brother who adored me and cared for me, made me stronger.

> —"Michelle Obama says her brother is still their mother's favorite," *Good Morning America*, November 13, 2018

AND I HAVE to be aware of what I say and how I say it because if you want to get a point across... if you're a woman and you're too angry people stop hearing the point. They don't hear you.

> —"Best of: Becoming Michelle Obama," *2 Dope Queens*, March 12, 2019

YOU KNOW, OF course my parents loved us, but my mother was like, 'There are a lot of other kids who were as smart as you, but the difference between success and failure when you're a woman, when you're a minority, is really slim.'

—"Best of: Becoming Michelle Obama," *2 Dope Queens*, **March 12, 2019**

WELL, YOU KNOW, it starts with looking back on those times when I was told that I couldn't do something before anybody even knew anything about me.

—"Best of: Becoming Michelle Obama," *2 Dope Queens*, **March 12, 2019**

THERE ARE FEW things that inspire me like seeing the potential of adolescent girls around the world.

—**Twitter, October 11, 2018**

THERE ARE MORE than 62 million girls around the world who are not in school—girls whose families don't think they're worthy of an education, or they can't afford it.... Girls like Malala Yousafzai who are assaulted, kidnapped, or killed just for trying to learn. And this isn't just a devastating loss for these girls, it's a devastating loss for all of us who are missing out on their promise.

—Let Girls Learn in London, June 16, 2015

IF THESE TEN women can endure death threats and horrifying violence and years behind bars to stand up for what they believe in, then surely our young people can find a way to stand up for what they believe in.

—on the ten honorees at the International Women of Courage Award Ceremony, March 8, 2012

WHEN WE VIEW [girls'] voices as equal, when we truly listen to them and appreciate what they say, they will feel more empowered to share themselves with the rest of the world, too.

—**Instagram, May 10, 2019**

WOMEN ARE DEFINITELY under a lot of pressure, but I think it's important to remember that to look good, you have to feel good. I look at my mom at 74 and see how beautiful she looks and how wonderful she is with our daughters and with me and my husband—and I want that for myself when I'm her age.

—***Prevention Magazine*, March 2012**

I BELIEVE EVERY girl on the planet deserves the same kind of opportunities that I've had—a chance to fulfill her potential and pursue her dreams.

—**Instagram, September 5, 2019**

The Next

Generation

WHEN WE TALK about the potential of our young people, we often think about it as some far-off promise, years or decades away. But the truth is they have so much to offer us right now.

—**Instagram, August 1, 2019**

WHEN I THINK about the issues facing our nation, I think about what it means for my girls, and I think about what it means for the world we're leaving for them and for all our children.

—**"Michelle Obama Hits Campaign Trail With Soft-Sell Message,"** *The New York Times*, **October 13, 2010**

WE ARE CURIOUS, creative beings. But it's also the work of parents, teachers, and community members to keep that flicker of curiosity alive. Because kids know what's up. They know when the adults around them have assumed failure as a foregone conclusion. A hurtful remark, an air of indifference—those things add up. And they can do real damage to a young person's desire to learn.

—*The National*, **Amtrak, August/September 2019**

WE MUST CONFRONT wrong and outdated ideas and assumptions that only certain young people deserve to be educated, that girls aren't as capable as boys, that some young people are less worthy of opportunities because of their religion or disability or ethnicity or socioeconomic class. Because we have seen time and again that potential can be found in some of the most unlikely places.

> —"The age of youth: Traveling abroad, First Lady Michelle Obama makes kids Topic 1," *The Washington Post*, April 15, 2010

IF ANY OF you are scared or confused or angry, or just plain overwhelmed by it all, if you feel like you're searching for a lifeline just to steady yourself, you are not alone.

> —"Dear Class of 2020" Commencement Address, June 7, 2020

NEVER EVER BE embarassed by those struggles. You should never view your challenges as a disadvantage. Instead, it's important for you to understand that your experience facing and overcoming adversity is actually one of your biggest advantages.

—commencement address at City College of New York, June 3, 2016

PEOPLE CAN ONLY define you if you let them. In the end, it's up to each of us to define ourselves. It's up to us to invent our own future with the choices we make and the actions we take.

—commencement address at Virginia Tech, May 14, 2012

STUDIES SHOW THAT those kinds of skills—skills like grit, determination, skills like optimism and resilience—those skills can be just as important as your test scores or your grades.

—Bell Multicultural High School, November 12, 2013

I'm not saying that grades aren't important, I'm just saying that they're less important than what you learn and what you're made of.

—commencement address at Martin Luther King, Jr. Magnet High School, May 18, 2013

AND THOUGH [MY great-grandfathers] didn't live to see it themselves, I can see the smiles on their faces knowing that their great-granddaughters ended up playing ball in the halls of the White House—a magnificent structure built by enslaved Americans.

—Instagram, June 19, 2020

KIDS DON'T COME to this earth jaded and racist and cynical and misogynist. They come here pure and open. We teach them all of that stuff.

—*The Late Show with Stephen Colbert*, December 1, 2018

THAT IS WHAT we're deciding. Not Democrat or Republican, not left or right, no, in this election and every election, is about who will have the power to shape our children for the next four or eight years of their lives.

—Democratic National Convention, July 25, 2016

OUR GREATNESS HAS never, ever come from sitting back and feeling entitled to what we have.... Our greatness has always come from people who expect nothing and take nothing for granted, folks who work hard for what they have then reach back and help others after them.

—commencement address at City College of New York, June 3, 2016

I LOVE HOW creative and confident Gen Z is, especially the young women. They're far more outspoken and driven than girls were when I was growing up—they don't as quickly cede ground to the boys or accept different treatment, and that's terrific. Technology has allowed their entire generation to learn and experience so much so quickly.

—*The National*, Amtrak, August/September 2019

YOUNG PEOPLE HAVE an especially important role to play—we need them at the table to truly move this country forward.

—Instagram, May 12, 2020

IF WE WANT to give all of our children a foundation for their dreams, and opportunities worthy of their promise, if we want to give them that sense of limitless possibility, that belief that here in America, there is always something better out there if you're willing to work for it, then we must work like never before.

—Democratic National Convention, September 4, 2012

WE HELPED CHANGE the culture around how our kids eat and how we move. We're seeing college graduation rates and high school graduation rates go up.

—"The Final Interview With The Obamas (Full Interview)," PeopleTV, December 20, 2016

WE'RE CREATING AN opportunity for these young leaders to go online, to learn, to get resources, to be trained, to talk to each other, to network.

—"Best of: Becoming Michelle Obama," *2 Dope Queens*, March 12, 2019

We have to feel that optimism. For the kids. . . . Progress isn't made through fear. We're experiencing that right now. Fear is the coward's way of leadership. But kids are born into this world with a sense of hope and optimism.

—*O, The Oprah Magazine,* December 2018

You guys are our future, and you have a President and a First Lady who love you to death. We love you like you're our kids and we want the absolute best for you. We want to expose you to the absolute best that this country and this world has to offer. And then we expect you to do great things with it.

—"Hamilton at the White House" workshop,
March 14, 2016

We've seen recently that the young and diverse America . . . is still here, still hopeful, and still blowing us all away.

—Instagram, July 7, 2020

THAT'S BEEN THE most powerful part of the last year—talking with all sorts of young people about how the things that we think are our inadequacies are usually our strengths. The simple act of sharing our fears and vulnerabilities helps us embrace our own stories and recognize how much we share with one another.

—*People*, December 4, 2019

PICK YOURSELF UP, dust yourself off, and keep moving through the pain. Keep. Moving. Forward.

—commencement address at City College of New York,
June 3, 2016

MY STORY CAN be your story. The details might be a little different, but let me tell you, so many of the challenges and the triumphs will be just the same.

—Bell Multicultural High School, November 12, 2013

MILESTONES

1964

- Michelle LaVaughn Robinson is born on January 17 in Chicago, Illinois to Marian Robinson and Fraser Robinson III. Marian works as a secretary at Spiegel, a catalog company that markets women's apparel, but later stays home to care for Michelle and her older brother, Craig. Fraser is a city-pump operator who is pressed into becoming a Democratic precinct captain to advance in his career. He has multiple sclerosis, which makes his mobility increasingly difficult—he walks with a cane when Michelle is young, which progresses to a crutch by the time Michelle finishes elementary school.

- Michelle grows up on the South Side of Chicago in a small apartment on the top floor of a bungalow on the South Shore. She sleeps in a shared bedroom with Craig, who is close enough in age—only 21 months older—that the children are often mistaken for twins.

- The Robinsons are a close and loving family who speak openly with the children about adult topics. Music is a central part of family life, and Michelle enjoys listening to her father's enormous jazz collection. Family meals are usually homemade, and her grandmother makes sure there are at least two vegetables on each plate. Dinnertime conversations are marked by lively debates and plenty of humor. Michelle credits her upbringing as teaching her the value of caring for community, working hard, sharing stories, and getting an education.

- The Robinsons teach Michelle and her brother to read by the age of four, and they both skip the second grade. Michelle goes on to study in a gifted program for sixth grade, where she is able to take French and advanced biology classes.

1981

- Michelle graduates as class salutatorian from Whitney M. Young Magnet High School for gifted children in Chicago. Named for a civil rights leader, it is the first public magnet school in the city, established in 1975 as part of the city's effort to comply with the Supreme Court decision desegregating public schools. The school is an hour away from the Robinson home by city bus, a route that Michelle takes twice a day to get to and from school.

- Michelle, who feels the weight of her parents' and grandparents' sacrifices to invest in her education, takes school seriously and strives for high grades and awards. During her time attending high school, she becomes a member of the National Honor Society, serves as the student council treasurer, and is accepted to her first-choice school, Princeton University, where Craig is already enrolled.

- A first-generation college student (both her parents had enrolled in community college, but did not complete their degrees), Michelle is put into an early orientation program at Princeton to help low-income and minority students prepare for college life. Ultimately, however, it is a difficult adjustment at the school, where the student body is mostly wealthy, white, and male.

- In Michelle's freshman year, she is assigned two roommates, both of whom are white. One of her roommates soon transfers to a single room, but Michelle does not learn until later that this is because the student's mother was upset that her daughter had been assigned a Black roommate.

1985

- Michelle graduates cum laude from Princeton University with a B.A. in Sociology and a minor in African American studies. In her thesis, "Princeton-Educated Blacks and the Black Community," she writes that her time at the school has made her more aware of her race than ever before.

- While at Princeton, she is a member of the Organization of Black Unity and an assistant at the Third World Center, which Michelle calls "poorly named but well-intentioned," providing a warm and welcoming place for minority students to connect and receive support. She also creates an after-school reading program for children.

- Michelle enrolls in Harvard Law School.

1988

- Michelle is awarded her J.D. from Harvard Law School. During her time at Harvard, she participates in demonstrations to promote diversity on campus and increase the enrollment of minority students. Throughout her time at law school, she works at Harvard's Legal Aid Bureau, providing legal assistance to those unable to afford attorneys, and she joins the Black Law Students Association to bring speakers to campus to bring awareness to legal issues and offer career guidance to students.

- After graduation, she begins working as an associate attorney specializing in intellectual property and marketing at Sidley Austin in Chicago.

1989

- Michelle is assigned to mentor Barack Obama, a summer associate and one of the only other Black attorneys at the firm. The firm pairs them in part because Barack is a first-year student at Harvard Law, Michelle's alma mater. Michelle is wary of him before he arrives, tired of her colleagues' excitement over the new intern, and when he shows up late to the first meeting, she is annoyed. But she likes him as they get acquainted. Barack asks Michelle out many times but she declines, concerned that a relationship with him would be—as she later says—"tacky," or might complicate their work together. After Barack offers to quit his job so she'll go out with him, she agrees to a date.

- On their first date, the couple sees Spike Lee's *Do the Right Thing*. Outside of a Baskin-Robbins ice cream shop, they share a first kiss. Michelle describes this as the moment she knew the relationship would become a serious one.

1991

- Michelle's father, Fraser Robinson III, dies at the age of 55.

- Following the death of her father, Michelle reevaluates her career in corporate law. Wanting to honor the values of her parents and follow the work she finds most rewarding, she dedicates herself to serving communities and neighborhoods. She continues to pursue public service throughout her career.

- Bolstered by her love of her hometown, Michelle takes a position as assistant to Chicago mayor Richard M. Daley. There, she works with Valerie Jarrett, whom she introduces to Barack. Jarrett would go on to become one of Barack's senior advisors and a high-profile part of his presidential administration.

- After her time in the mayor's office, Michelle becomes assistant commissioner of planning and development in Chicago's City Hall.

- Michelle and Barack become engaged.

1992

- On October 3, Michelle and Barack are married at the Trinity United Church of Christ in Chicago. They recite their own vows and dance their first dance as a married couple to Stevie Wonder's "You and I." The couple honeymoons on the California coast.

- The newlyweds move into an apartment in Chicago's Hyde Park neighborhood.

1993

- Michelle becomes the Founding Executive Director of the new Chicago chapter of Public Allies, an AmeriCorps program established during Bill Clinton's administration. This youth leadership training program equips young adults with skills needed for careers in public service, a mission that is close to Michelle's heart. While at Public Allies, she goes door-to-door recruiting youth for the program and sets impressive fundraising records that stand for over a decade after her departure.

1996

- Michelle leaves her position at Public Allies to become the Associate Dean of Student Services at the University of Chicago. She is also Director of the University Community Service Center, where she works to further develop the school's first student-run community service organization. In her new role, Michelle provides students with service opportunities throughout the city of Chicago. During her time working at the University of Chicago, the volunteerism rate on campus soars.

- Although she is initially against Barack entering politics due to her distaste for politicians and the instability of political life, she actively supports his campaign for Illinois State Senate, which he wins, by canvassing for signatures and fundraising.

1998

- On July 4, Michelle gives birth to the Obamas' first daughter, Malia. Though she doesn't reveal it publicly until the publication of her memoir in 2018, the couple had struggled with infertility, and Michelle had had a miscarriage before Malia's birth, after which they turned to IVF treatments to conceive.

1999

- While campaigning for the Democratic primary for Illinois's First Congressional District, Barack stays with Malia, who is very ill, and misses a vote on a major bill. The backlash he receives from opponents for staying home to care for his sick infant fuels Michelle's frustration with politics.

2000

- Michelle supports Barack throughout an unsuccessful primary challenge to United States Representative Bobby Rush, which Barack later calls "an ill-considered race." He loses to his opponent, a former Black Panther leader with great local popularity, by more than 30 points.

2001

- On June 10, the Obamas' second daughter, Natasha (known as Sasha), is born.

2002

- After taking four-month-old Sasha to an interview at the University of Chicago Hospitals, Michelle is offered a position as Executive Director of Community and External Affairs. As her career accelerates and Barack tends to legislative business away from home, Malia and Sasha remain Michelle's biggest priority, and she seeks out ways to maintain a good work-life balance. She goes on to speak about the importance of support and flexibility in the workplace for working families throughout her career.

2004

- Barack is elected to the United States Senate, taking office in 2005. Michelle is active in his campaign, and the election, along with Barack's popular speech at the 2004 Democratic National Convention, brings national attention to the family.

- At the Democratic National Convention, minutes before Barack walks on stage to deliver what would become a breakout speech, Michelle offers her husband words of encouragement: "Just don't screw it up, buddy." When asked for comment about her husband's performance at the Convention, she steadfastly responds with understatement: "Must've been a good speech."

2005

- Michelle is promoted to Vice President of Community Relations and External Affairs at the University of Chicago Medical Center, where she works to improve access to medical care and encourages the hospital to adopt new practices to support all patients, such as hiring patient advocates.

- With the intention of bringing the hospital's services to the communities of Chicago, Michelle begins serving on the boards of the University of Chicago Laboratory Schools and the Chicago Council on Global Affairs.

- While seeking to gain experience in corporate management, Michelle is elected director on the board of TreeHouse Foods, Inc., a food manufacturer and distributor, where she serves on the audit and corporate governance committees.

2006

- When Barack's candidacy is first discussed, Michelle joins the strategy meetings. She has concerns about how the campaign will raise enough money to compete with Hillary Clinton and other primary candidates and demands a concrete plan from Barack's advisors.

2007

- Michelle resigns from her position on the board of TreeHouse Foods, Inc. She cites the inability to effectively split her time between her family, the campaign, and her professional responsibilities, although some speculate that the company's ties to Walmart clashed with her husband's opposition to their labor practices.

- Michelle reduces her hours at the University of Chicago Medical Center to become more involved in Barack's campaign leading up to the state primaries, speaking to groups across the country.

- In October, she participates in the first forum of political spouses ever held, gathering nearly every spouse of Democratic and Republican presidential candidates at the Women's Conference in California.

2008

- Michelle plays a major role in Barack's 2008 presidential campaign. In her speaking engagements, Michelle connects with her audiences by sharing her own stories and life experiences, drawing connections between those experiences and her husband's campaign goals. She gains a reputation as being blunter than her husband, which allows her to address more divisive topics and voice frustrations that Barack is less willing to discuss. This cements her place in the public eye and opens her to increasing criticism from voters, the media, and political opponents.

- While campaigning, Michelle leaves Malia and Sasha with her mother, Marian. She sometimes delays speeches so she can talk to them on the phone, a fact that she shares with her audiences. "Thank God for Grandma!" is a refrain on the campaign trail.

- At a campaign stop in February ahead of the Wisconsin primary, Michelle thanks supporters for the groundswell of support they have given Barack and his plans for change in Washington. In an impromptu moment, she tells the audience, "For the first time in my adult life, I am really proud of my country because it feels like hope is finally making a comeback." These words are quickly levied against her and her husband's candidacy, as critics suggest the couple is radical and un-American. Though she clarifies and walks back the statement, it is a difficult moment that follows Michelle throughout the campaign.

- Michelle delivers a speech at the Democratic National Convention that is praised by media outlets and wins admiration from the public that reflects in the polls. Adept at gaining the support of undecided voters at campaign stops, she earns the nickname "the closer" within the campaign.

- Although she continues in her role at University of Chicago Hospitals during the primary campaign, Michelle switches to part-time work, both to accommodate her work on her husband's campaign and to allow her to spend more time with her daughters. She eventually takes a leave of absence.

- During an interview on The Tonight Show hosted by Jay Leno, Michelle appears in a gold skirt and matching cardigan over a silk blouse. When asked about where she bought the outfit—which had been chosen in response to a recent revelation that Sarah Palin, then the Republican vice-presidential candidate, had a campaign clothing budget of $150,000—Michelle proudly responds, "J. Crew." The moment vaulted the retailer to newfound popularity and resonated with women across the country, who admired both Michelle's style and frugality. Throughout her time as First Lady, Michelle's fashion choices—often bold and revealing of her personality—are followed with a fervor likened to that devoted to Jacqueline Kennedy.

- Barack wins the presidential election and in his victory speech, he thanks Michelle for the sacrifices she has made, the resilience of her support in his campaign, and for being "the rock" that grounded their family.

2009

- On January 20, Michelle becomes the First Lady of the United States, also becoming the first Black First Lady in American history. She identifies three main objectives on which to focus during her tenure as First Lady: help working parents find a healthy work-life balance, provide support to American military families, and encourage a rise in community service.

- Michelle begins her outreach as her husband begins his presidency, visiting homeless shelters, soup kitchens, and schools. Her favorability ratings are about 75 percent, up from 43 percent during the campaign, rising especially among groups that had previously criticized her.

- Michelle's highest priority in the White House is taking care of her daughters while living under the scrutiny of the public eye. In their early life at the White House, the Ty Inc. toy company introduces new dolls named "Sweet Sasha" and "Marvelous Malia." Michelle is displeased with the company using her daughters' names for marketing, and Ty Inc. quickly discontinues the dolls.

- In March, Michelle facilitates the creation of the White House's first vegetable garden since Eleanor Roosevelt's Victory Garden. She is inspired not only by Roosevelt but also by the stories of her grandmother tending a victory garden in Chicago when Michelle's mother was a child. The White House Garden, which consists of various vegetables and herbs, is planted and harvested by elementary students in the area to educate them on food and to reap the benefits of their labor. She also has beehives installed to encourage pollination.

- Michelle serves on the board of directors of the Chicago Council on Global Affairs.

- ABC's Barbara Walters names Michelle her "most fascinating person" of the year. In the accompanying interview, Michelle describes the most difficult part of her job as First Lady as the "constant concern" that she is doing enough to make the country proud. She also states that although Barack would have given up his political career if she had asked him, she thinks that she made the right decision in supporting him.

- Although she often positions herself as a mother and wife first, Michelle is engaged in politics. She hosts a White House reception for women's rights activists to mark the enactment of the Lilly Ledbetter Fair Pay Act of 2009, supports the economic stimulus bill, and makes plans to visit all Cabinet-level agencies as she accustoms herself to Washington.

2010

- Michelle campaigns for Democrats in the midterm elections.

- After a surprising discussion with her pediatrician, who raises concerns about her daughters' weight gain, Michelle decides to focus on health and nutrition—not just for her kids, but for kids nationwide. She launches her Let's Move! campaign to address childhood obesity by helping schools provide healthier meals, encouraging kids to be more active, and supporting parents' efforts to make healthier choices for their children.

- *Forbes* names Michelle Obama the most powerful woman in the world.

- Michelle appears in *The Hooping Life*, a documentary to promote hula-hooping for health.

- Barack signs the Healthy, Hunger-Free Kids Act, a bill which reauthorizes many child nutrition programs through 2015, including the National School Lunch and Breakfast programs and the Special Supplemental Nutrition Program for Women, Infants and Children (WIC). Michelle praises the passage of the bill as foundational to the work of her Let's Move! initiative.

2011

- Michelle launches the Joining Forces initiative along with Dr. Jill Biden. This initiative is intended to support veterans, service members, and their families by educating the public about their experiences, fostering a connection between the general public and military families, and developing wellness, education, and employment opportunities for service members and their families. It is largely successful, especially in the area of increasing employment for both veterans and military spouses.

2012

- Barack wins reelection and remains President for a second term. Michelle is more involved in his campaign than she was in 2008. Although still seen as a polarizing figure, she is considered more popular than her husband, with an open and approachable persona.

- In May, Michelle and Barack announce their support of same-sex marriage. This is Michelle's first time commenting on the issue.

- Michelle publishes *American Grown: The Story of the White House Kitchen Garden and Gardens Across America*, which documents her experience with the White House Garden throughout the season and the connection between health and quality food.

- At the site of Michelle and Barack's first kiss outside the Baskin-Robbins in Hyde Park, a plaque is installed on a 3,000-pound boulder to memorialize their love.

2014

- Michelle launches the Reach Higher initiative to help students pursue their education beyond high school, with a special focus on low-income and first-generation college students. The initiative highlights college access and financial aid resources, exposes students to career and summer learning opportunities, and supports school counselors who work directly with students.

- Michelle works together with the FDA to make changes to nutrition labels on food. The new changes include making calorie counts bigger and bolder, listing added sugars, and making serving sizes more proportionate.

- Michelle makes a guest appearance on *Parks and Recreation*, playing herself.

2015

- Michelle and Barack launch Let Girls Learn, an initiative dedicated to helping improve adolescent girls' access to education worldwide through a broad variety of programs and public-private sector partnerships. During press events announcing the initiative, Michelle shares stories of young girls from around the world who have overcome poverty, violence, and other obstacles to attain an education, citing them as inspiration for the work.

- Michelle, along with her daughters and mother, stay at Kensington Palace and have tea with Prince Harry. Michelle and the Prince discuss helping military families as well as the Let Girls Learn initiative.

- Welcoming thousands of athletes, Michelle kicks off the Special Olympics World Games in Los Angeles.

- After the landmark Supreme Court decision Obergefell v. Hodges, which legalized same-sex marriage throughout the United States, the administration honors the decision with a rainbow light display projected on the White House. In her 2018 memoir, Michelle reveals that that night, she and Malia, then 16 years old, snuck out of the residence past Secret Service agents to witness the public's emotional celebration.

2016

- Along with endorsing Hillary Clinton, Michelle makes several campaign speeches both with and for her. Her efforts are unprecedented—no sitting First Lady has ever campaigned so prominently for a former political rival, much less a former First Lady.

- Michelle holds her last garden-planting event at the White House, a tradition established to help educate kids on the importance of healthy foods. She ends the event by saying she hopes the subsequent administrations uphold the tradition of feeding and educating children through the garden.

- Michelle Obama appears in a one-on-one interview with Oprah Winfrey on a special, "First Lady Michelle Obama Says Farewell to the White House," in which she reveals her belief that her husband's administration achieved its goal of giving hope to the American people.

2017

- Michelle and Barack move out of the White House and retire their titles of President and First Lady.

- In her parting remarks as First Lady, Michelle says serving the country was the greatest honor of her life.

2018

- Michelle publishes her memoir *Becoming* on November 13, which details her life's journey from Chicago to the White House. It quickly becomes a #1 *New York Times* Best Seller.

- She is voted the woman most admired by Americans according to Gallup's annual survey, removing Hillary Clinton from the spot for the first time in 17 years.

- Marian Robinson, when asked in an interview what about her daughter made her proudest, says, "When I grow up, I would like to be like Michelle Obama."

2019

- Gallup names Michelle the most admired woman in the world for the second year in a row.

- The *Michelle Obama: Forward Motion* documentary is created to showcase Michelle's life journey from Chicago's South Side to the White House.

- In response to racist tweets from Donald Trump against Alexandria Ocasio-Cortez, Ayanna Pressley, Ilhan Omar, and Rashida Tlaib—the four congresswomen of color often referred to as "the

Squad"—Michelle tweets, "What really makes this country great is its diversity."

2020

- Netflix releases *Becoming*, a documentary about Michelle's tour for her book of the same name.

- Michelle begins a PBS KIDS Read-Along Series on TV called "Mondays with Michelle Obama," where she reads her favorite children's books to kids.

- In July, Michelle launches *The Michelle Obama Podcast*, with Barack as her first guest.

- The *Becoming* audiobook wins Michelle a Grammy for Best Spoken Word Album.

- Michelle and Barack serve as executive producers on *Crip Camp: A Disability Revolution*, a documentary about a summer camp for teens with disabilities, many of whom went on to become activists in the disability rights movement of the 1970s.

- Michelle and Barack reveal they are working on producing a Netflix series called *Listen to Your Vegetables & Eat Your Parents* to teach young children and parents about the origins of health food around the globe.

- It is announced that Viola Davis will star as Michelle Obama in the upcoming Showtime drama series *First Ladies*.

Acknowledgements

We would like to thank Kelsey Dame, Emily Feng, Paige Gilberg, Rachel Hinton, Marilyn Isaacks, Eva López, Claire Maclauchlan, Elizabeth Pappas, Briana Rooke, and Suzanne Sonnier for their invaluable contributions to the preparation of this manuscript.